WALL STREET: THE OTHER LAS VEGAS

EXECUTIVE ORGANIZATION
OF
THE NEW YORK STOCK EXCHANGE

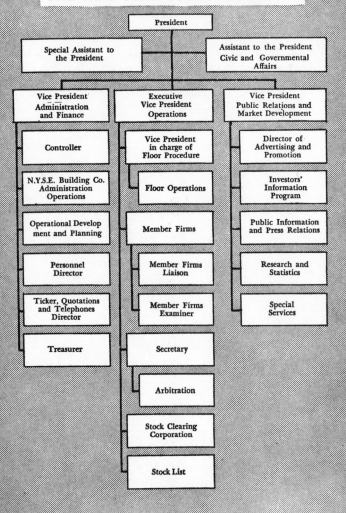

President

Special Assistant to
the President

Assistant to the President
Civic and Governmental
Affairs

Vice President
Administration
and Finance

Executive
Vice President
Operations

Vice President
Public Relations and
Market Development

Controller

Vice President
in charge of
Floor Procedure

Director of
Advertising and
Promotion

N.Y.S.E. Building Co.
Administration
Operations

Floor Operations

Investors'
Information
Program

Operational Develop
ment and Planning

Member Firms

Public Information
and Press Relations

Personnel
Director

Member Firms
Liaison

Research and
Statistics

Ticker, Quotations
and Telephones
Director

Member Firms
Examiner

Special
Services

Treasurer

Secretary

Arbitration

Stock Clearing
Corporation

Stock List

ORGANIZATION CHART OF A CASINO

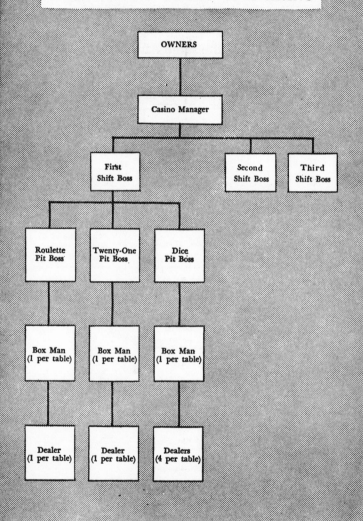

OWNERS

Casino Manager

First Shift Boss | Second Shift Boss | Third Shift Boss

Roulette Pit Boss | Twenty-One Pit Boss | Dice Pit Boss

Box Man (1 per table) | Box Man (1 per table) | Box Man (1 per table)

Dealer (1 per table) | Dealer (1 per table) | Dealers (4 per table)

By the same Author:

*How I Made Two Million Dollars
In The Stock Market*

Nicolas Darvas

WALL STREET: THE OTHER LAS VEGAS

Lyle Stuart
Kensington Publishing Corp.
www.kensingtonbooks.com

LYLE STUART BOOKS are published by

Kensington Publishing Corp.
850 Third Avenue
New York, NY 10022

All Kensington titles, imprints, and distributed lines are available at special quantity discounts for bulk purchases for sales promotions, premiums, fund-raising, educational, or institutional use. Special book excerpts or customized printings can also be created to fit specific needs. For details, write or phone the office of the Kensington special sales manager: Kensington Publishing Corp., 850 Third Avenue, New York, NY 10022, attn: Special Sales Department, phone 1-800-221-2647.

Designed by Sandra Lee Stuart

First Kensington Printing: February 2002

10   9   8   7   6   5   4   3   2   1

Printed in the United States of America

Cataloging data may be obtained from the Library of Congress.

ISBN 0-8184-0398-5

WALL STREET: THE OTHER LAS VEGAS

Contents

Preface

*T*EN YEARS AGO I bought my first share of stock. Four years ago I added up my winnings. I had made $2,000,000 in the stock market.

A publisher asked me to write a book about it and I did. More than 400,000 copies of *How I Made $2,000,000 in the Stock Market* were sold.

Its impact was so great it caused the American Stock Exchange to change its rules.

I was invited by one of the largest Wall Street investment banking and brokerage houses to form a Darvas Mutual Fund.

A politically ambitious Attorney-General, encouraged by unhappy brokerage houses, began a front-page "investigation" that ended in the obituary columns when I agreed not to sue him for libel and he and I agreed that I wouldn't act as a broker.

I have received thousands of letters. Almost everyone wanted tips and advice, and I kept saying to these

11

people, "I don't necessarily know how *you* can make money. I only know how *I* made it and continue to make it." My publisher suggested that I write a second book about my experiences and observations of the stock market.

I decided to do just that; for since I started in the stock market more than a decade ago I have learned other things besides the making of money.

Standing back and observing the scene I began to see Wall Street as it really was—a gambling house, peopled with dealers, croupiers and touts on one side and winners and suckers on the other. I had been a winner and was determined to stay one. So I began to acquaint myself with the workings and the workers, the myths and the mysteries that swirled around this second—but bigger—Las Vegas.

I reckoned the odds and learned how to cut down on them and this is my story:—one gambler against the biggest gambling house in the world.

Now let us enter the Casino. . . .

NICOLAS DARVAS

Georges V
Paris, France 1963

CHAPTER ONE

The Casino

THE SCENE is the crowded Oak Room of the fashionable Plaza Hotel in New York. Cocktail time, May 28, 1962. Outside, heels click smartly along Central Park South. Traffic roars. Inside, surrounded by people in animated conversation, I am quiet. I sit in my favorite corner, opposite the door, sipping a Planter's Punch, doing a little mental arithmetic.

On the margin of the newspaper on my table, I write a sum, and enclose it in a neat rectangle in bright blue ink:

$$\$2,450,000.00$$

Nearly two and a half million dollars. Incredibly, that is the amount that I had realized in Wall Street in just seven short years. By far the greater part of it,

$2,250,000, was made in just eighteen months! It hardly seemed possible.

I should have become used to the idea of being a millionaire by now. I had already written a best-selling book about my Wall Street experience. I had been the subject of fantastic publicity—articles in *Time* magazine; in *Barron's*, the bible of Wall Street. Slick magazines had published cartoons about the "dancer wizard" of the stock market. Comedians and columnists and commentators and the amazing sale of my book had made my name familiar to an audience which had never seen my dance act at the Latin Quarter in New York, or the Coconut Grove in Los Angeles.

It had been a fascinating, wonderful game, with some amusing highlights—like the time I found myself without change in Reuben's and gave the head barman, Warren, a tip on the stock market instead of the seventy-five cents I had intended to give him. The tip was on AUTOMATIC CANTEEN. He bought it at 31⅝, sold it at 40, and made a profit of about $800. Not a bad tip, at that!

I had even stirred up a hotbed of controversy. Was it really possible for a layman like myself, a dancer who admittedly hadn't known a put or call from a bump or grind when he started, to plunge in where expert economists feared to tread—and come out two million dollars ahead of the game?

It was not only possible; it had happened. And other things happened too. The American Stock Exchange altered its rules and suspended the use of stop-loss orders, apparently to curb speculators trying to play "Follow the Leader"—or "Follow the Dancer" in this case.

But all of this was water over the dam. What had triggered my memory into action, as I sat in the Oak Room on that May evening of 1962, was the front page of the newspaper on which I had just made that neat little notation of my net assets. And what I was really thinking was, "Darvas, you are a lucky man."

Not just because I happened to have money in the bank. There was a closer connection. Screaming up at me in big, black type from the front page of the *New York Post* were the words:

STOCKS PLUNGE
WORST SELLING WAVE
IN THIRTY YEARS

The headlines were the epitaph of a phase of the biggest and longest bull market in Wall Street history. For perhaps a couple of million small investors who had not even realized that they had been gambling, the headlines spelled absolute disaster. Thousands of accounts were wiped out by what looked, during this first day of the 1962 landslide, like the crash of 1929 all over again.

But the May crash was even bigger than the *Post* indicated in its first edition after the New York Stock

Exchange had closed for the day. I found out that $20.8 *billion* of so-called "paper values" were erased from the Big Board in a single day, and $40 *billion* lost within a week!

And it was only the beginning. After a brief rally, the down escalator picked up speed. Many stocks, like the $600 blue chip, mighty IBM, did not really hit bottom until well into June. People I talk to still have not recovered.

Yet while the storm of selling shook the stock market like an Alpine avalanche and even brokers went broke, there I sat sipping a cool drink, and able to read the headlines with perfect detachment. Because—here is the remarkable fact—I was already well *out* of the stock market.

I had closed the last of my brokerage accounts more than four months earlier!

It was something to think about. It was no coincidence. It had not just *happened* that way. Yet, on the other hand, I could claim no credit as a prophet. No crystal ball. No tea leaves. No tip-off from esoteric charts and graphs, no help from Wall Street insiders.

The simple truth was that it had not mattered even slightly whether I, Nicolas Darvas, as an individual had been able to anticipate the May crash or not.

I was aware of the approaching avalanche, *as early as December,* and I had begun to close out my stock holdings *automatically*—without my having to lift a finger!

There had been no excruciating, do-or-die decisions to make. My stop-loss orders, carefully adjusted to my "box" system of stock buying which I had learned to use, had made my decisions for me. If I persisted against the tide, and bought back into the market after being sold out, the stop-losses again tripped the automatic safety controls at the first downward fluctuation and, click, I was out again.

So here I was, four and a half months after my last venture in Wall Street, at my usual table in the Oak Room reading in the *New York Post* that, once again, the Big Wheel of Wall Street had hit double zero. Once again the insiders were picking up the chips at bargain basement discounts; once again the people from Main Street, U.S.A, were running panic-stricken, with what they could salvage from the latest Wall Street disaster.

I don't think that there was any complacency in my sentiments. Yes, I was happy. I had picked up my chips and left. Who wouldn't feel fortunate? But at the same time I began to think of my fellow players in the Big Casino—as I had learned to regard the Big Board.

Did they understand what was going on? Did they know it was a game? A sweepstake? That one had to play to win, but be prepared to lose. Did they know it could be a financially fatal pastime?

It was not until after I had made my own stake in the stock market that I had even considered such questions. Now, realizing the seriousness of the crash for

17

millions of people who had gambled but could not afford to lose, I decided that I wanted to tell the whole story, as I knew it, as it happened to me. A compulsion to describe this glittering casino which is bigger than Monte Carlo and makes Las Vegas look like a has-been took hold of me. I wanted to tell the story of my experiences.

It would be, I decided, a way of showing Wall Street for what it really is: a professional gambling casino, filled with losing and winning gamblers (which traders actually are).

According to the Securities and Exchange Commission report which has just been released, there are about 17,000,000 owners of stock in the United States. The figure is slightly misleading.

In the first place, not everyone who owns a share of stock in a corporation is actively "in" the market. Most are not. Stock owners can be divided roughly into two classes: those like myself who buy and sell, and those who merely happen to be sitting on nest eggs, mostly small ones. The nest-egg sitters include:

Some millions of employees of big corporations like GENERAL ELECTRIC who own a few token shares in the companies they work for—usually purchased at a discount. (Smart labor relations on the part of the companies, but it does not make much difference to the stock market, as we shall see.)

Executives who enjoy stock options as a means of

spreading out their income (usually after retirement) and so beating the tax collector.

The legion of those who have been lucky enough to inherit a few blue chips from some provident aunt and are happy to have an occasional dividend check.

With the possible exception of the executives, these people don't speculate. They rarely buy; they seldom sell except in a real personal emergency. I can think of acquaintances, and no doubt you can, too, in this category.

For example, I know a girl who works as a sales representative for PAN AMERICAN WORLD AIRWAYS. She owns 100 shares of PAN AM stock. Recently, perhaps because of talk of a possible merger between PAN AMERICAN and TRANS WORLD AIRLINES, the stock began to show a little life, for the first time in months. My friend, Miss X, had bought it at 20. In January of this year it was around 27. Suddenly it began to add points. When it reached 32, I asked her whether she was thinking of selling, and taking a profit.

"Oh, no," she said. "It brings me a nice little dividend check every so often, and, anyway, as long as I'm working here, it's nice to have some Pan American stock."

But sentiment sometimes means more than money. As I remarked earlier, not everyone who owns stock is actually "in" the stock market.

Another friend of mine came to ask my opinion

about some shares of stock his wife had inherited from an uncle. What was the stock? SIBONEY CORPORATION, an oil exploration company with oil and gas leases in Cuba, listed on the American Stock Exchange.

Unfortunately, the SIBONEY stock had been purchased in about 1957 B.C., meaning Before Castro. Currently, SIBONEY was selling at ¼, or 25 cents a share, with few takers.

Here is another example of a stock owner—one of the estimated 17,000,000—who is not, for any practical purpose, in the market.

People like these probably make up the majority of all of those who own shares in American corporations. They don't buy, they don't sell, they don't gamble, and—what is most important to Wall Street—they pay no commissions. Sometimes they collect dividends; in other cases, as above, they merely hold the stock.

But it is with those who *do* pay commissions, and who hope to make some money in Wall Street, that both the stock brokerage community and this book are mostly concerned—though for different reasons.

I have found that, oddly enough, the widows and orphans who traditionally are supposed to live on dividends from blue-chip stocks *are* in the market, although usually by proxy. That is, their money is either in mutual fund shares, or in the hands of trust fund managers who supervise their "portfolios" for a fee.

Either way, there is a periodic readjustment of the

"portfolios," which means selling some stocks and buying others to replace them. What this comes down to is betting that one stock is about to fall in price, that another is about to rise. To put it plainly, the widows and orphans are gamblers, too, along with a host of others—although they don't actually place their own bets.

Because I became fascinated with all facets of the casino I looked up some figures. I found that the number of people actually gambling on the market varies. It includes (1) more than 105,000 individuals buying shares on the New York Stock Exchange's Monthly Investment Plan, at the rate of $40 a month or more. The M.I.P. is for people who can't afford to put a substantial lump sum into the stock they happen to want, and who, in many cases, have been persuaded that rising prices will pay the rather steep commissions involved in buying stock on the installment plan.

(2) Some 3,000,000 mutual fund share owners. As indicated above, they let someone else place their bets for them. The gambling is conducted by the professionals who manage the funds. The individual's only gamble is whether his mutual share will be worth what he paid for it when he wishes or needs to sell it.

(3) The so-called "odd-lot public." This is made up of people who, for various reasons but usually because of limited resources, buy stock in quantities of less than 100-share "round lots."

21

It is hard to say how big the odd-lot public really is.

One of my broker friends tells me that about 60 per cent of the business of his large office consists of the transactions of small buyers dealing in broken lots of less than 100 shares. That is, it *was* about 60 per cent of the business, before the May 28 crash.

Even fairly well-heeled investors are not always sufficiently affluent, or confident, to buy 100 shares at a time in such stocks as XEROX, at this writing selling at 416; or IBM at 510. Who buys 100 shares of SUPERIOR OIL at $1435 per share?

For example, in December 1962 the number of odd-lot *sales* topped the number of odd-lot *purchases* by 2,659,092 shares—an all-time monthly record. That's a lot of selling on the part of small investors, and it indicates just what you would suppose—that as of December, the small fry who had been "locked in" by the May price collapse were now fleeing from Wall Street.

All the little fish add up to a very big business—as we shall see when we come to the question of brokerage house profits.

Will the small fry return? The late J. P. Morgan is credited with a classic remark concerning the only certainty of the stock market, namely: "It will fluctuate."

I should judge that Morgan's terse yet ponderous pronouncement must also apply to the gambling public which supports the stock market. In its comings and goings, it, too, "will fluctuate."

Is a New Bull Market
Now Under Way?

The teaser from an investment tip service advertisement leaps out at me from the financial section of the *New York Times*. It is not a new ad, nor a new question; I've been seeing it for some months now, even when the market was at a dead standstill, and the volume was down near the 3,000,000 mark.

What is the answer?

Frankly, I don't know. No more than I know where the roulette wheel will stop in a casino in Las Vegas. The fact is that the tip service operators don't know either, or they would be retired millionaire traders, not operators of a $5-a-throw tip service.

The history of Wall Street, however, shows one very clearly that the market, like the economy in general, (but not concurrent with it) has its cycles of boom and bust. After a bust it is about time to expect some improvement. Prices go down, prices go up. The losers leave, cleaned out. New gamblers eventually appear.

The really important questions for me, however, were: (1) how can I make money in the market? and (2) how can I protect myself from loss? I have made money in the Casino. I have beaten the odds. This is the chronicle of my adventures—of my assault on this money fortress, this glittering gaming table, this greatest of all lotteries.

In the beginning . . .

I have been called a gambler, and in a sense that is true. Everyone who puts down X number of dollars in the hope of picking up X plus a profit is, in a sense, gambling.

But I can say that from the beginning, my idea was to eliminate the element of risk, or to cut it down as much as possible. I liked winning. Who doesn't? But at the same time I was conservative by nature; when I saw the figures on the stock market ticker tape go down a point, down two points, three points, my heart sank with it; I was terrified!

Because of that fear, I eventually evolved some personal guidelines. When I was engaged in this game my main consideration was to lose as little as possible.

But this is to anticipate something that did not develop for quite a while. In the beginning, I took a lot of chances. And the worst of it is that I took them without even understanding that I was gambling. I started off with some strange ideas about the market, and a strong dose of overconfidence—which had to be cured before I could begin to learn anything.

My first venture into the market came about by pure chance, not in Wall Street, but in Canada. I was offered a block of Canadian mining stock in an unusual business deal, as payment for a dancing engagement in Toronto, instead of cash. I couldn't take the engagement— at the time I was dancing in the Latin Quarter in New York, and I had other commitments.

But I did buy the stock which had been offered, and became, to my surprise, the owner of $3,000 worth of something called BRILUND.

BRILUND? It sounded like a new kind of kitchen cleanser. I considered it with distrust. Then I put it aside and forgot about it for a while, being busy and on the move, with engagements in Madrid and elsewhere.

When I next looked at a newspaper stock market column, more from idle curiosity than for any good reason, I was staggered. There was BRILUND, jumping out of the page at me. I had bought it at 50 cents a share. The quotation in the newspaper was $1.90! For a moment I was sure that it must be a misprint. BRILUND which you might have mistaken for a soap powder and actually represented some unlikely mining venture in the Canadian bush, had nearly quadrupled in value!

I sold at once. My original $3,000 had by some miracle became over $11,000. And as you might expect, I was hooked. From here on in, I was going to be a big stock market operator. Judging by the *Brilund* experience, the market certainly looked like the primrose path to easy millions.

I felt like a man who had been let in on a big secret. I was filled with confidence and a sense of power. No one had told me anything about stocks or the market but, now that I knew of the existence of these things, I believed I had found the key to financial success. It was merely a matter of finding a reliable broker, choosing the right stock, and my experience with BRILUND could be repeated again and again, indefinitely.

Why didn't everyone get in on this wonderful invention, the stock market? Well, that was their affair, not mine. I began to look around for other good stocks. Where? People with money ought to know and, since I worked in nightclubs where I often met such people, I could ask—and did.

Everyone had a tip, a rumor, inside knowledge, a favorite stock which was sure to go up. It seemed that the existence of the stock market was not such a well-kept secret, after all. But when I began to back some of the tips I picked up, with my own money (the working capital which BRILUND had given me), I began to realize that the road to a fortune in the stock market was not so wide open as it had appeared.

In the next year I tried dozens of ventures, looking for another BRILUND. I had started in the Canadian penny market, and it was natural that I should stay there, trying to repeat my initial coup. The results were nil. I found myself reversing the merchandising slogan, "A profit in pennies," by *losing* pennies in the thousands on stocks with such unlikely names as OLD SMOKEY GAS AND OILS, REXSPAR, KAYRAND MINES.

My records at this time would have discouraged any but the most optimistic newcomer to the market: Bought at 19 cents, sold at 10 . . . bought at 12, sold

at 8 . . . bought at 130 cents, sold at 110 cents. . . .
When I balanced my brokerage account, I found that
my losses were averaging $100 a week, dribbling away
in pennies—and in brokerage commissions on losing
transactions.

My buying was completely haphazard. I was like a
neophyte gambler who has been allowed to win a
little something as a come-on, and continues to plunge,
long after the tide has turned, sure that if he persists
he will hit the lucky combination again. Oddly enough,
I was far from discouraged. I was sure that it was
simply a matter of finding the key, so to speak, to the
mysteries of profitable buying and selling in the stock
market.

That I had a long way to go was evident. Even the
elementary matter of brokerage commissions was
Greek to me at the start, as will be seen from the following experience.

Having done well with BRILUND, I was on the look-
out for another good mining stock. Someone suggested
KAYRAND MINES. Mining what? Money, I had hoped.
I hadn't the slightest idea what the name represented,
but the stock was selling at 10 cents a share, which
certainly looked like a bargain. To make a long story
short, I bought 10,000 shares. Price $1,000.

A thousand dollars was a lot of money to me, even
granting that I was still quite a few thousand dollars
ahead from my original streak of good luck with BRI-

LUND. It was a gamble, and I watched KAYRAND MINES with the emotional intensity of a school teacher playing a 30-1 shot on her first visit to the race track.

Sure enough, KAYRAND MINES was mining something. Within 24 hours the price had risen to 11 cents.

If I had been traveling, instead of on the scene, I might have let it ride, praying that it would turn into another BRILUND while I was looking the other way. Being all too close to the market, I was not enough of a gambler—too conservative by nature—to take a chance for long. Unconsciously, my reasoning followed the Wall Street proverb, "You can never go broke taking a profit."

Don't you believe it!

Here is my arithmetic as applied to KAYRAND MINES:

```
10,000 shares purchased @ 10¢  = $1,000
10,000 shares sold @ 11¢       = $1,100
                    PROFIT        $  100
```

Unfortunately, I had overlooked a small but vital detail, the brokerage commissions. My broker gave me the bad news. His commission for buying 10,000 shares of KAYRAND MINES was $50. Oh, yes, and for *selling* 10,000 shares, another $50.

Subtract the two commissions, plus a small transfer tax, and I had almost—but not quite—broken even, by "taking a profit."

In truth, it was my broker who had taken the profit, to the extent of $100, for the trouble of placing a couple of telephone calls. How could he lose, with clients like me to pay his rent?

It took me a long time to learn how to stop this steady erosion of my working capital, brought about by the drip, drip, drip of brokerage fees and transfer taxes on my numerous timid, small-profit (or small-loss) transactions.

Even after shifting my operations to New York and Wall Street (Hurray! the big time at last!) I continued to jump in and out of the market like the star performer in a flea circus. And of course each gyration was the occasion for another round of discreet but undoubtedly sincere applause from my broker, who had every practical reason to approve.

My records for July of 1954, a year and a half after my venture in KAYRAND MINES, illustrate the problem which I continued to face, once committed to a career as an amateur speculator in Wall Street. The records indicate the purchase and subsequent sale of stock in four major corporations:

AMERICAN BROADCASTING-PARAMOUNT

NEW YORK CENTRAL RAILROAD

GENERAL REFRACTORIES

AMERICAN AIRLINES

The first two registered gains of a point or less. I sold to take a quick profit.

The other two declined slightly, and I sold at once, lest they continue to lose ground and cost me real money.

The four transactions involved, altogether, the sum of $19,311.41. By this time I was in for a lot more than the original $3,000 with which I had innocently bought BRILUND, plus the BRILUND profit of nearly $8,000 which I had thought to pyramid into a fortune. The truth is that I was operating out of my own pocket, and barely holding my own. Total changing hands on four stocks: $19,311.41. When I had finished adding and subtracting gains and losses, I found myself with a net profit of just $1.89!

My broker, meanwhile, had pocketed commissions totaling $236.65.

Well, a profit was better than a loss, even if it was only $1.89. Actually I was very much ahead of the game, because by this time I had finally learned my first important lesson in the stock market. It was to be a guiding principle with me from then on, summed up in three short words!

Stop that leak!

In other words, find a way to cut down those brokerage commissions, by avoiding the kind of hit-and-run, small-profit operation that only the floor-trader member of a stock exchange, paying no commissions, can afford to make.

I have heard traders in the American Exchange speak of "taking an eighth here, picking up an eighth there," meaning one-eighth of a point, or 25 cents per share, on quick in-and-out transactions in relatively small quantities of low-priced stocks.

This is the sort of thing members of an exchange can do. *I cannot.* I pay a commission when I buy, another commission when I sell. In addition, there is the transfer tax. If I trade in odd lots, there is also the odd-lot broker's one-eighth or one-quarter per share profit, above the price on the board. It all added up. The more transactions I engaged in, the happier my broker was—and the less money I was likely to make, even in the best of bull markets. His commission may not be high—according to the New York Stock Exchange, it averages out to about 1 per cent—but there is such a thing as being nickeled to death, and in the stock market it can happen a lot faster than I dreamt.

I have been speaking of the stock market collectively as a lottery, a gambling enterprise, a casino. This is no mere figure of speech. The average reader may say, well, sure, we understand that there is a certain element of *risk* in buying stocks; even the brokers admit that.

But no—I am speaking not merely of risk, but of gambling in the fullest sense of the word, the same sort of gambling you will find in Las Vegas, where you bet on the turn of a card, or the movement of a little ivory ball spinning around a numbered wheel, or when you put your $5 or $50 on the Big 8 at the dice table.

In Las Vegas, the owners of the casinos have a direct interest in the spin of the wheel, the turn of the card. They are betting their money against yours. The percentages, naturally, are in their favor; if not, they would not remain in business.

Now, here is the fact as I have observed it. The stock market is not appreciably different, except in one important respect: it is the broker-members of the stock exchanges who own the Wall Street casino; and although some of them bet their money consistently against the public's, most of the profits of the brokerage community as a whole come not from gambling, but from commissions.

Brokerage commissions are the primary reason for the existence of the organized stock exchanges; without the brokerage commission, there would be no Wall Street casino.

This I realized early in the game and I wasn't gulled by the propaganda relating to "sound investments," "shares in American business," and the like which gushes forth continually like Niagara from the pens of copywriters.

I must grant that the hucksters of Madison Avenue have done a good job of selling Wall Street to Main Street, for a purpose which may be perfectly legitimate. But I don't misunderstand that purpose: it has very little to do with shares in American business; the primary purpose is to bring more gamblers into the casino to buy and sell more stocks and generate more commissions for the brokers who own and operate the casino.

I have no pretensions to sainthood. What I do have is a lively interest in *facts*, as these relate to my income, and it is a fact that "people's capitalism," as depicted by the New York Stock Exchange, is largely a myth. The "people," meaning the vast majority of the population of the United States, own a very small part of the capital instruments of the free enterprise system; in fact, public ownership of the means of production is not greater but less extensive than it was a century ago.

As regards corporations, it is true that they are initially financed, and that industrial expansion is financed to a greater or less extent, by the sale of stock to the public. What then? The management of the corporation, having received its share of the proceeds from the underwriters, has little to do with that particular issue of stock in the future—except as the corporation officers may own shares in the company.

A stock that is initially offered at $30 may fall in price to $5 a share, or rise to $150 as it passes from hand to hand in the market place. Since it is not redeemable, like a bond or a promissory note or a mutual fund share, it makes no difference to the corporation what the price of the stock may be. The company's financial affairs do not depend on the fluctuations in the market, but on more practical matters, entirely unrelated to those handsomely engraved certificates which bear its name.

Dividends? There is no obligation. The board of directors will vote to pay dividends, or not, at its own discretion. If the directors own a big block of the stock themselves, as is usually the case, they may want to pay dividends.

On the other hand, there may be lots of good reasons why they will *not* wish to pay. They may be more interested in expansion, in acquiring the assets of other companies through stock trades, in building a financial empire and creating high-priced executive jobs, in the control of wealth for its own sake.

Meanwhile, dividend or no dividend, the stock of the corporation will continue to be traded in the market. And here is the truth of the matter: *it will be traded largely on the basis of the buyer's estimate of how much he may subsequently be able to sell it for.* This is speculation, this is the gamble.

What it amounts to is that, when you buy a $10 or a $20 or a $50 stock, you are paying $10, or $20, or $50 for a nicely printed certificate and wagering that someone else will pay more for it than you did. And, of course, that someone else who takes the printed certificate off your hands will be making exactly the same kind of bet.

The commission broker's part in the whole affair

will be, naturally, to stimulate lively betting and collect as many commissions as possible. He is, in case you didn't know, one of the owners of the casino in which the bets are placed. And his membership gives him the privilege of taking a cut on each transaction that he handles. After all, this is the reason he joined the casino; it is the reason he, or another member of his firm, was willing to lay out $40,000 for a seat on the American Exchange, or upwards of $150,000 for membership in that exclusive gambling club—the New York Stock Exchange.

Business is business, it has its ups and downs, and involves some risks. No one ever claimed it was a sure thing. But the risks are usually calculated risks, the up-cycles and down-cycles are both explicable in rational terms. The coal or fuel oil business is fine this year because we had a cold winter and people burned a lot of fuel. The melon business is dismal this summer because farmers grew more melons than people care to eat and melons are a glut on the market.

The gambling business—and this describes Wall Street—is something else again. It is not rational, and the proof of it is the wild fluctuations of stock prices, not merely from day to day but from hour to hour. The rising and falling prices on the stock market ticker tape resemble nothing so much as the runs of good and bad luck, of sevens or elevens or deuces and treys at the dice table.

If a share of stock is, as the New York Stock Exchange copywriters like to say, "Your Share in American Business," why should its price change twenty times a day?

Does the price of my dinner from fluctuate one evening to the next? Suppose that when I went to the Oak Room in the Plaza for cocktails, as I often do, the bartender were to say:

"Good evening, Mr. Darvas. Martinis are being quoted at 97 cents this evening, sir; Manhattans 78; bourbon 43; the bottom has fallen out of sweet vermouth and it's down to 3; but the dry is holding firm at 39; club sandwiches $5.26; pickles $1; and I don't recommend the chicken salad until we see how the proxy fight in the kitchen is going to come out."

A ridiculous world, if it were so. I see a valuable property at 650 Park Avenue. I don't see real estate being quoted on a ticker tape: 650 Park Avenue going for $3,500,000 in the morning, three hours later selling for $3,530,000, two hours later down to $3,450,000, the next day only $2,900,000. I don't see the man who sold it at three o'clock one afternoon rushing in the following morning to buy it back for less than the price he received for it the day before.

To suggest that such fluctuations of price in any commodity could serve the public interest is insane. But in *gambling*, naturally, it is another matter. Fluctuations in the value of numbers in a lottery is necessary to the entire existence of that kind of lottery, and one gets what one pays for—a gambler's chance to sell numbers; or, in the case of Wall Street, symbols printed on paper IP—INTERNATIONAL PAPER, CN—NEW YORK CENTRAL, IBM—INTERNATIONAL BUSINESS MACHINES, GM—GENERAL MOTORS, for more than one paid for them.

An example from those above, IntBusM, meaning INTERNATIONAL BUSINESS MACHINES: a glance at the charts which any broker has in his office will show that the price of IBM between 1936 and 1960 ranged all the way from 3⅞ per share to 400. In 1961 the low was 387; the high, an amazing 607! In 1962 its peak price was 587½ in January, down to 300 in June, up to 392½ by the end of December. At this writing it is selling for about 510.

The IBM chart for a year is on page 38.

At the same time the company's earnings were per share:

1961	7.52
1962	8.72
1963	(estimated) 10.00

Each year was better than the previous year. Then why the insane price swing?

Even a moment of reflection will suggest that charts like that are illogical. Swings indicated on the price chart have no relationship to INTERNATIONAL BUSINESS MACHINES as a business enterprise. The price roller coaster relates only to the fluctuations of the price of

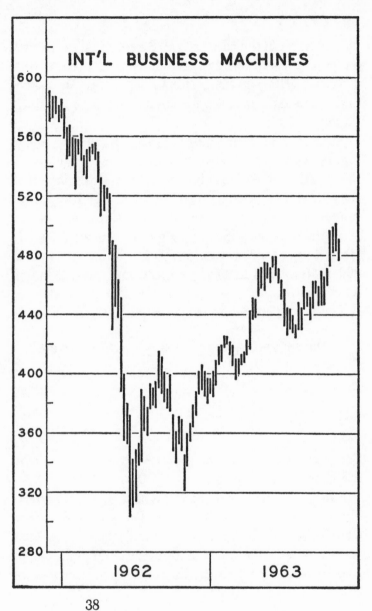

INT'L BUSINESS MACHINES

IBM in the Big Casino known as the New York Stock Exchange.

A glance at my newspaper shows me that IBM pays an annual dividend of $4 per share. That is something less than 1 per cent at current market prices, and I don't have to tell you that no one invests his money to earn 1 per cent.

The plain truth is that people who buy IBM—at $300, or $600, or at any price—are simply betting that it will rise in price. The same applies to most speculative stocks and, as far as I am concerned, practically all common stocks are speculative stocks. They may go up, they may go down. Take a chance, and find out.

If I seem to belabor the point about gambling and the stock market, it is not with bluenose intentions, but to *underscore the essential realities of the situation!* My experience in the market has taught me that there is only one rational way to approach the business of buying and selling stocks for a profit; and that is, first of all, to understand very thoroughly what it is that I am buying and what it is that I hope to sell again.

The ABC's of Wall Street, as I have found it, are these:

A. When I buy stocks I am buying chips in a casino.

B. My object is to take advantage of the price fluctuations created by the speculation of my fellow gamblers in such a way as to get more for my chips than I have paid for them.

C. But since that is also the object of the other players, I must be very sure that I play my game well.

The first lesson that I learned in the stock market has already been told on pages 26 to 29, in connection with my venture in KAYRAND MINES. It was the fact that, contrary to the Wall Street adage, I could go broke taking a profit—if I took it too soon and too often. The reason is, obviously, the broker's commission, which comes off at each end of a transaction, whether I won or whether I lost.

The bite is small, as percentages go, but it is constant, and thus it is the one big item of overhead, the daily "admission" I pay to gamble in the Wall Street casino.

As I dug a little deeper into the market I saw that the commission broker was the dealer—and a clever one—in the Wall Street casino.

CHAPTER TWO

The Dealers

*t*HERE were serious prob-
lems I faced during my first year or so in the stock
market. My basic problem, now that I look back on it,
was my misconception of the nature of stocks, the
market, and the role of the men who operate it.

To begin with, I had been told that a share of stock
was a share in the actual ownership of a business
corporation, that the *value* of such shares increased or
declined with the relative prosperity of the corporations concerned, and that the stock market was oper-
ated primarily to provide the financing that these
companies required. "Own Your Share of American
Business," is the New York Stock Exchange slogan.

It seemed simple enough, until I thought about it.
For a brief time I bought stocks hit or miss, on tips, on

41

hunches; if I wanted to console myself I could say that I had been "getting the feel of the market."

But now I decided that, since stocks represented shares in business, the obvious thing to do was to make a thorough study of business—find out which industries were strongest, which companies most promising, and then buy the stocks of those companies. If a given industry was flourishing, and a corporation within that industry growing and prospering, it logically followed that its stock must go up in price.

I saw nothing wrong with this logic. It told me, as plainly as ABC, that the best shares to own would be those in the biggest, strongest, and richest companies of the biggest and most prosperous industries.

Confidently I set out to make a choice based on facts, this time—instead of guesswork—and almost immediately ran into a roadblock.

A study of the stock tables in back issues of *Barron's* weekly financial newspaper, comparing prices from week to week over a period of a couple of months, showed me something that any broker could have told me, had I asked.

It was that the shares of the best established companies, those with the most capital and earnings and the longest record of paying dividends, were precisely the stocks that fluctuated *least* in price. Some of them—and this was especially true of the preferred stocks—seemed not to move at all. No change, no profit. I seemed to be barking up the wrong tree.

My study of price movements also showed me that stocks with equal ratings in terms of dividends, earnings, safety, and similar factors might often behave quite differently from one another. Of three stocks that seemed absolutely identical from every point of view, two might stand still or even decline, while the third would show an unexpected rise of several points —for no sound reason that I could see. Obviously there were factors that I wasn't able to take into account. But these were not listed in any guidebook or annual report.

However, there was one clue, and it seemed a promising one. I had noticed that, although so-called quality was, in itself, no sure indication of which way a stock would go, stocks did bear some relationship to one another. They were not traded in an absolute vacuum. In particular, I could see a sort of follow-the-leader tendency in the various *industry groups.* This observation seemed to be confirmed by the daily stock market reports, especially those that I heard on radio each evening.

"Oils led the market today," I would hear. "Standard Oil of New Jersey was up five-eighths, Socony gained a quarter, Sinclair added three-eighths, non-ferrous metals declined slightly, but textiles were firm . . ." and so on. It seemed to me, listening to such reports and studying them in the *Wall Street Journal,* that this was the way the market moved, first one group gaining,

43

then another pushing to the top, like schools of dolphins surfacing one at a time.

If one stock in a given group gained a point or so, others in the same group seemed to benefit from this activity. I could only guess at the reason, but in any case the observation seemed to have some merit.

I had been poring over company reports, financial statements, tables of dividends, figures on price-to-earnings ratios, margins of profit—all the so-called "fundamentals" of stock trading.

Now it began to appear logical to suppose that my best bet would be to pay some attention to the way in which the various *groups* of stocks as a whole were behaving. I should select the most active and strongest group, I reasoned, then choose the leader of that group, and I could hardly go wrong. All it required was close attention to details, a careful analysis that I now felt confident of my ability to make. I was beginning to be my own market expert.

In due course I found what I was seeking. The name of the stock was JONES & LAUGHLIN STEEL. It was in a key industry if not *the* key industry in the entire American economy, and ranked close to the top in that industry in terms of earnings, rate, and record of regular payment of dividends, and similar "fundamentals." Yet it was selling at what seemed to me to be a reasonable price, and when I compared it point by point with other steel stocks, it checked out favorably against stocks selling for 10 to 20 points higher.

The steel industry as a whole was showing a great deal of strength in the market, and I felt that it would be only a matter of time before JONES & LAUGHLIN must have its rightful share in the general prosperity. From every point of view, it appeared to be a great bargain.

By this time I was so convinced of the soundness of my reasoning, so eager to "get in on the ground floor" before others became aware of it, that I would almost have bet my life on JONES & LAUGHLIN. What I did do was close enough to it.

I telephoned my broker and gave him the order to buy 1,000 shares, on margin. The price averaged out to 52½ per share. With the 70 per cent margin requirement then in force, the total cash that I had to deposit came to $36,856.61. It represented virtually everything I had in the world. It was all my capital and all I could borrow; my salary was pledged for weeks ahead, and some property I owned in Las Vegas was mortgaged; I was "in" the market up to my neck and would certainly drown if my calculations were wrong.

The strange thing is that I was not at all anxious. The "fundamentals" that I had studied so painstakingly told me that JONES & LAUGHLIN was due for a rise. By my arithmetic, it was *worth* at least $75 a share, and I waited confidently for it to assert its true value.

It seemed almost immediately that my calculations were wrong. Something was amiss somewhere. JONES & LAUGHLIN was *worth* $75 a share, maybe, but it seemed

45

that other speculators did not think so. They quite evidently did not consider it worth even the 52-½ per share that I had paid for it.

Three days after I gave the order to buy, JONES & LAUGHLIN began to slip. First it dropped by fractions, then by whole points. With each point down, I lost $1,000.

Once there was a brief rally, a little flutter of life. Then the stock continued on its tortuous downward course, off ⅛, off ½, off 1, off 2.

Within three weeks, it had sunk to 44—8¼ points below the average price I had paid!

As far as I was concerned, it had touched bottom. I had had it. I sold—for a loss of $9,000, including commissions and interest on my margin loan.

It was quite clear to me now that there had been something gravely wrong with my whole approach to the market. The logic that had seemed so persuasive simply had not applied to reality. I had had better results in my earlier phase, when I had been taking out and out gambles, without the slightest knowledge of "fundamentals." Going over my reasons for buying JONES & LAUGHLIN—a strong B+ safety rating in Standard and Poor's book, a dividend near 6 per cent, good annual earnings, and so on—I still could see nothing wrong with my original reasoning. It *was* a good company in a strong industry. The stock *was* a bargain, compared with stocks selling for much more. But it

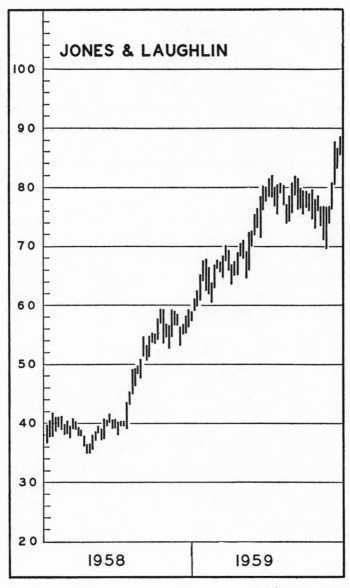

JONES & LAUGHLIN

had not gone up, it had gone down. Where had I gone wrong?

I didn't know, but I did know that I had to do something to recoup my loss. I began to study the stock tables in *Barron's* and the *Wall Street Journal* again, seeking clues to the mysterious motions of the market, the unpredictable daily and hourly rise and fall of prices on the Big Board. If it was not fundamentals, what was it?

My attention was attracted, finally, to a stock called TEXAS GULF PRODUCING. Producing what? I did not even know that much about it. But what I did notice, checking the prices over a period of weeks, was that, where some stocks seemed to bounce up and down like ping-pong balls and others merely stood still, changing hardly at all, TEXAS GULF PRODUCING had been steadily rising.

Surely that was what was important, if anything was. I had no sound reason to suppose that *Texas Gulf Producing* would continue to rise in price, but neither did I have any reason to suppose that it would not. Once again I was gambling, but this time, at least, I was like a racetrack bettor who has learned to pay some attention to form. *My* horse—TEXAS GULF PRODUCING—had been winning races. That was something. I decided to take the plunge.

I bought in at $37\frac{1}{4}$.

The next day, the price was 38—a gain of 75 cents

per share—and I had a thousand shares. A first-day gain of $750.

I held on, mentally shouting, *"Come on, Texas Gulf Producing!"*

Slowly, it continued to gain—38¼, 38¾, 39, 40. When it slipped back a fraction, my heart sank. This really was like a horse race! When it crept ahead again, I could hardly keep myself from selling, for fear that it would again lose ground. Finally, at 43¼, a solid six points ahead of the game, I decided that I had taken as much of a gamble as I cared to do.

I telephoned my broker and told him to sell. My winnings, less commissions and transfer tax, came to more than $5,000.

At the time I could not have told you whether the TEXAS GULF oil wells were spouting petroleum or Grade A milk, but what was certain was that I had recouped more than half of my loss on JONES & LAUGHLIN, a company with whose affairs I was extraordinarily well acquainted.

TEXAS GULF PRODUCING! It had produced a profit. That was the one sure thing I knew about it. *Why* it had risen when other stocks in the same group with equally attractive fundamentals had stood still remained a complete mystery to me.

No doubt there were reasons. It could be that insiders, who knew more than I could know about the stock, were buying; obviously *someone* was buying,

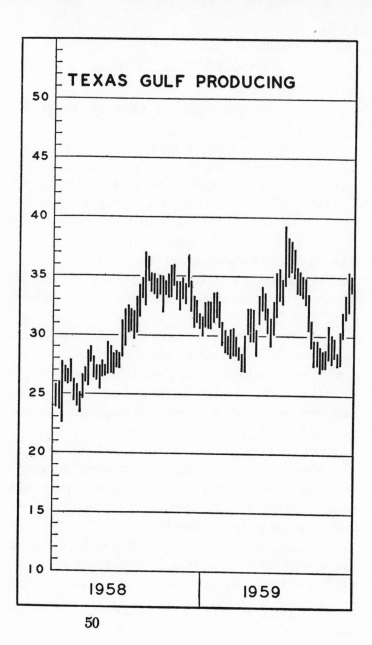

TEXAS GULF PRODUCING

or there would be no rise in price. But I decided that if there were reasons, they were the sort of reasons of which I could know nothing, until it was too late.

Naturally I would continue to take an interest in the strength, prospects, and financial condition of companies whose stock I might consider buying. But these factors in themselves could never tell me whether to expect the fast and substantial profits I sought.

My primary approach, then, would have to be to act on the indications of the market itself, as seen in the daily stock price tables, and in a careful study of previous price movements. In other words, I would scrutinize the field for likely winners on the basis of previous form and actual performance. Breeding, training, the reputation of the jockey and the kind of oats the horse was eating were all very good things to know. But my first rule would be to bet only on the horse that was running out in front. If and when he weakened, well, then I would get off and look for another front-runner.

I still had not found any scientific way of picking winners, but I had begun to get a glimmering of my theory, and I had learned an important lesson. It was simply this:

Business is one thing; stocks are another. As I had seen, an industry or a corporation can boom while its stock busts, and it was possible, as far as I could tell, that the same thing could happen in reverse. In any event, I could plainly see that there was no sure key to stock market speculation in the prized economic indicators recommended by the brokerage community.

I had received a valuable clue to the nature of the stock market. In the future, I resolved, I would simply have to forget about my Share of American Business, and treat stocks like what they seemed to be for all practical purposes: white, red, and blue chips in a giant gambling casino.

How much was a given stock "worth"? I had learned that Standard and Poor and similar guidebooks could tell me nothing about that. For my purposes, a stock was worth exactly what I had to pay for it when I bought, and exactly what I could get for it when I cashed in my chips. As for good stocks and bad stocks, there were no such things; there were only stocks increasing in price and stocks declining in price.

A share of stock, whatever relationship it may have to the corporation that issues it or the industry that it represents, has no intrinsic value other than the amount that it will fetch in the market, based on the simple law of supply and demand.

This was the pragmatic approach to the market, for what it was worth. For me, at least, it proved to be worth a great deal, in plain dollars and cents. At the time, I was too busy to concern myself with questions about market theory. I did not ask "Why?"

Since then, however, I have made a thorough re-examination of my stock-market philosophy, and I have reached some conclusions that are confirmed privately by a great many professional traders—although there are good reasons why the latter don't want to talk about these conclusions.

The first is that the New York Stock Exchange slogan, "Your Share in American Business," is pure ballyhoo, designed for no other purpose than to persuade the American public to bet its hard-earned dollars on the uncertain performance of the red, white, and blue chips of which I have spoken before, the so-called "shares" of corporate stock.

The second is that the entire purpose of the vast enterprise known collectively as "the stock market" is, from the point of view of the men who run it, to churn up the greatest possible amount of buying and selling, so as to generate the greatest possible number of commissions.

I do not intend to argue, by any means, that the corporate practice of issuing stock has no other function than to provide chips for a lottery. Obviously the sale of stocks is a valuable way of financing new enterprises and, to a limited extent, of paying for the expansion of established enterprises.

It is all the more valuable because it is a painless way of sharing the *risk* involved in any business enterprise. If the enterprise succeeds, very well. The corporation may reimburse the shareholder by declaring a round of dividends. On the other hand, it may not.

It is surprising to discover how many companies, particularly those whose stocks are sold "over the counter," *have never paid any dividends.*

If the enterprise fails? Forget it. I will have bought some handsomely printed certificates, to prove that I have done my part for the national economy. I could keep them as souvenirs of my gambling days.

Of course, not very many of the corporations whose stock is listed on the Big Board are likely to fail—the New York Stock Exchange is an exclusive club, for million-dollar companies only. Most of them pay some dividends fairly regularly; they must, in order to retain their listings. Yet even here, the New York Stock Exchange record itself shows me that the average is less than impressive. In 1961, the average paid on common stocks listed on the Big Board was only 3.3 per cent. I could have done better at almost any savings bank. And this is to speak only of common stocks that actually paid a dividend. Many did not.

The whole process is very convenient for the corporations that sell the stock. It is summed up in a cynical Wall Street aphorism: "Why go broke? Go public."

Just what does that mean?

It means, as I see it, that the corporation gets the money it needs, absolutely free and clear of any obligation to repay it—ever. The underwriters get their cut or commission (or both) for placing the stock issue. The stockbrokers who handle all subsequent transactions in the stock get their commission. And the public

will get "shares" (i.e., chips) with which to gamble—
the gamble being, of course, that someone else will
pay you a profit on them in the hope of selling them to
a third person for a little bit more, and so on in an
endless cycle of speculation.

This is, in essence, the entire story of the stock
market, as I have found it. Like the South Sea Bubble,
the great tulip trading mania in Holland, the Ponzi
swindles, and the chain letters of the Depression, it is
kept in motion by one thing—faith. Sometimes the
chain is broken, confidence lost, the whole house of
cards comes tumbling down, and we have another
Wall Street crash. Then it starts all over again.

Fortunately for speculators like myself, there are
several factors—not present in Ponzi schemes and
chain letters nor in gambling casinos in Las Vegas—
that help to stabilize the Wall Street brand of gambling. They assure a relatively quick recovery after
each successive stock market boom has reached its
inevitable bust.

One of these factors is that a great many small investors (and some large ones as well) do not buy stocks
for the purpose of making a quick killing. They buy
for the dividend income offered, and partly as a hedge
against inflation—the theory being that when inflation
sends the prices of commodities up, the price of stocks
will also rise. Such buying provides a steady market
for common stocks—especially after a break in which
stock prices are depressed.

Investment trusts also tend to be active after a market collapse, buying in at the bottom, and thus helping to put stock prices back on the up escalator. And then there are the independent floor traders—broker-members of the stock exchange—many of whom consistently bet against the general public, selling stocks short when the public is buying, buying when the public is selling and prices are down.

That last has given rise to another cynical Wall Street saying, namely, "The public is always wrong."

The brokerage community, however, does its best to keep such sayings from reaching the ears of the public. In fact, the best Madison Avenue copywriting talent that money can buy is employed to convey an impression exactly the opposite of the adage quoted above. I was amazed to learn just how much money is spent on advertising.

How much? A single brokerage house, Merrill Lynch, Pierce, Fenner & Smith, Inc., in 1962 spent a cool $3,360,000 for advertising and public relations. When the firm's year-end report came, showing a decline in revenue because of lower market volume than the previous year, it was accompanied by the announcement that Merrill Lynch planned to *increase* its advertising budget for 1963 by another $1,000,000!

Advertising pays. Without it there would be much less public participation in the market. And without the public—little trading, no commissions.

The New York Stock Exchange says that brokerage commissions average out to about 1 per cent. This refers to commissions on the purchase of so-called round lots of 100 shares or more. Odd-lot commissions run higher.

The 1 per cent figure doesn't sound like much. To tell the truth, when I first got into the market, in Toronto, I actually did not realize that the broker to whom I was introduced charged *any* commission.

It simply did not occur to me to ask myself where his profit came in. I was too much concerned with my own profit, if any; and besides, the entire market was a mysterious phenomenon as far as I was concerned.

In general, the brokers with whom I have had dealings have managed to make me feel that they are Good Samaritans—there to help me, even at the cost of a good deal of inconvenience to themselves. Good old Charlie! Always at the other end of the telephone when I want to buy, or to sell. Always ready with advice. In fact, the one bit of advice which I didn't hear from my friendly broker was: "Do nothing." Get out of the market. That would be too much to expect. Brokers and their account executives are, like casino operators and croupiers, necessarily in business to make money. And on Wall Street, that means commissions.

Commissions are seldom mentioned between broker or account executive and client, but they are, of course, tacitly understood. To talk about the broker's end of the deal would be in slightly bad taste—rather like asking one's family physician, "How's business, doc?"

But my own arithmetic, confirmed by available statistics on the subject, shows me that the broker's 1 per cent adds up to a billion-dollar business, when multiplied by the millions of shares of stock traded daily, five days a week, on the New York Stock Exchange, the American Exchange, and the various smaller regional stock exchanges (to say nothing of the huge over-the-counter market).

The broker's commission is to Wall Street what the gambling house "cut" is to an organized poker game—the kind in which a professional dealer takes so much from every pot.

Like the card dealer, the broker is always there, cutting the pot, a little bit when you buy, another little bit when you sell. It follows that the more action there is, the greater the total of commissions, and the more cash in the house "kitty."

Let's see how all this works out in practice, in the nation's biggest stock market casino.

The price of stocks listed on the New York Stock Exchange ranges from about $2, the recent price of a share in MADISON SQUARE GARDEN, to more than $1,300 for a single share of SUPERIOR OIL. With some 1,300 separate issues listed, the average share currently costs about $40. And at last report, the daily volume of trading in the New York Stock Exchange—I am speaking of round lots of 100 shares—was running to about 5,000,000 shares changing hands.

$$5,000,000 \text{ shares} \times \$40 = \$200,000,000$$

One per cent of $200,000,000 equals $2 million a day in commissions—unless there is something wrong with my arithmetic.

Is there? There certainly is! If my friend the commission broker gets 1 per cent on the average for selling my stock, there is also another broker (if not the same one) who gets 1 per cent from the man who *buys* my stock. Thus the 1 per cent becomes 2 per cent and the brokerage community as a whole is knocking down a cool $4 million daily, 250 trading days of the year, as the house cut on all the gambling on all of the stocks—pardon, Shares in American Business—listed on the Big Board.

If I discount a healthy 30 per cent for transactions on which no commission is paid—namely, the purchases and sales of specialists, floor traders, and other members of the exchange—then add 15 per cent for odd-lot transactions, which don't appear on the ticker tape, the take is so large that it puts the Las Vegas "Strip" to shame.

This is just the Big Board. There is also the American Exchange, with a volume running well over 1,000,000 shares a day, and a dozen smaller exchanges, all of them put in the shade by the so-called over-the-counter market in no fewer than 70,000 separate issues of unlisted stocks.

I was interested in knowing where a brokerage house like Merrill Lynch, Pierce, Fenner & Smith stands in relation to its clients, the corporate giants of America, in terms of profits. This is what I found:

CORPORATION PROFITS FOR 1961

MERRILL LYNCH $22,000,000

Alleghany Ludlum Steel	$11,690,000
American Airlines	7,278,000
American Smelting & Refining	21,420,000
American Viscose Corporation	9,763,000
Chrysler Corporation	11,138,000
Container Corporation of America	18,200,000
Curtiss-Wright	5,970,000
Douglas Aircraft	5,957,000
Great Northern Railway	18,632,000
Hershey Chocolate	19,800,000
Illinois Central	12,715,000
Montgomery Ward	15,859,000
Northern Pacific	16,313,000
Otis Elevator	21,898,000
Philip Morris	21,511,000
Polaroid	8,111,000
Standard Brands	18,715,000
United Airlines	3,693,000
United Fruit	8,921,000
Western Union	12,226,000
Zenith Radio	18,015,000

For Merrill Lynch, that 1 per cent commission, marvelously compounded, added up to a whacking $22,000,000 NET profit for 1961. In 1962, the firm's net was only a little more than half the 1961 figure, and the reason was plainly stated in the company's annual report; a big drop in volume following the May crash.

With 540,000 clients, a staff of 8,700 employees, including 2,054 account executives and no fewer than 125 vice presidents, and branch offices in more than 100 cities, Merrill Lynch is far and away the world's largest brokerage house. Yet it is only, after all, one of many—and it is that 1 per cent average commission, the Big Casino's cut on every pot, that keeps the entire industry alive.

Merrill Lynch is not the Salvation Army, nor is my friendly stockbroker a social worker. His business, however much he likes you, is to generate commissions, and his advice to buy, sell, switch, "balance your portfolio," and so on must all be judged accordingly.

I find there is an important difference between the dealer in a gambling casino and the stockbroker. The difference is that the dealer usually works for a salary, and doesn't mind seeing anyone win, so long as we don't break the bank and put the dealer out of a job. The broker, on the other hand, has a direct stake in the amount of a customer's purchases and sales. If there is a profit, splendid. He'll be back. The important thing to the broker is that there is activity—buying, selling, and paying of commissions.

I learned another thing. It was exciting to jump in and out of the market for small profits—I got the sensation of important activity by doing a lot of trad-ing. Nothing pleased my broker more; he never said no to a switch. But I found I lost even when I was winning.

Before I learned to discipline myself, I had a number of experiences in which quick transactions for small profits of a point or two added up to absolute red ink on the balance sheet at the end of the month, when I took into account my operating overhead.

Even an honest card dealer can give bad advice, and, in this same connection, some of the brokers I have known are even less reliable, having an ax of their own to grind.

For example, in 1955, at a time I was just getting into the swing of trading in New York, an engagement called me out of town for a month, and, having con-siderable confidence in the broker who was handling my transactions at that time, I decided to give him authority to act on my account, to the amount of $10,000. I told him to use his discretion.

He did. It was a year in which the postwar vogue in aluminum stocks was dominating the market. Alumi-num was the metal of the future! Everything was going to be made of it—not only airplanes, but buildings, automobiles, furniture, baby carriages, for all I knew, billiard balls. The entire world was going to be re-fashioned of aluminum, and talk of this sort was sending the price of aluminum stocks sky high.

Smith bought aluminum. Then he sold it. Then he changed his mind and bought back in again. When I returned after a month I found that he had engaged in the following transactions on my behalf:

Bought KAISER ALUMINUM at 49, sold it at 51, bought it back again when it briefly dipped to 48, sold again at 49, abandoned aluminum in favor of SCHERING CORPORATION (pharmaceuticals) at 22, sold it at 28, returned to KAISER at 60, sold at 62, then went back to SCHERING to take another small profit of a couple of points, and again sold—while both KAISER and SCHERING continued to push upward, with no ceiling in sight!

Meanwhile, as I learned to my dismay, Smith had put a part of my $10,000 in a railroad stock that he favored, buying it at 28, and holding it while it fell off point by point to 27, 26, 25, 24. . . .

Altogether, he had made about 40 purchases and sales on my behalf, dipping in and out of the two stocks that were rising on the market, while clinging grimly to the one that was falling! He was out of both KAISER and SCHERING when I returned, but was still holding the railroad stock, as it continued to fall. I had to *order* him to sell it, and even then he protested, saying, "Don't worry, it'll come back."

The reason he had sold the aluminum and pharmaceuticals stocks was "to take a profit." And conversely, he had kept the declining railroad stock because he didn't want to present me with a loss!

As a matter of fact, I showed an over-all profit—of about $300.

Smith showed an over-all profit, too. His commissions totaled $3,000.

If he had bought KAISER ALUMINUM *and held it,* the situation would have been reversed. The broker would have earned $150 in commissions, and I would have received the $3,000 which he got.

Perhaps another stockbroker would have handled my affairs more for my benefit and less for his own. But, as I have said, the broker's business is to generate commissions, and you can't really expect him to put your interest before his necessity.

The Wall Street saying, "You can't go broke taking a profit," is absolutely true—for the dealers. Smith convinced me of that.

He had also taught me a lesson from which I made a rule for myself that was to pay off handsomely in the future.

I never sell a stock while it is rising. Why get off a winning horse? *And I never hold one that is declining.* Why stay with a loser? There will be time enough to ride him when he pulls ahead of the field.

CHAPTER THREE

The Croupiers

LIKE ALL GAMBLING GAMES and virtually everything else that involves money and the element of chance, the stock market can be rigged.

Just as croupiers have been caught running crooked wheels, powerful men of Wall Street have been tripped up in some very malodorous deals. One Exchange President, Richard Whitney, rhapsodically described the stock exchange as "a perfect institution. A God-given market." Mr. Whitney's enthusiasm was possibly premature. His brokerage firm was suspended from trading on the New York Stock Exchange because Whitney had "misappropriated" $5,662,000 of his customers' money.

But both casino operators and Wall Street operators believe strongly in their ability and right to police their own house, and Wall Street has managed, over the past thirty years, to get by with relatively few major scandals. The powerful public relations batteries of the brokerage industry generally succeed in glossing over the lesser scandals and in preserving and embellishing the industry's image of super-respectability.

Since 1934 the Securities and Exchange Commission has been considered the "Watchdog of Wall Street." Wall Street has never really got used to the idea. As Will Rogers said, "Those boys on the street sure don't like the idea of a cop on their corner." However, the Securities and Exchange Commission, even when reporting on grave faults in a system affecting the fortunes of millions of investors, is careful not to impair public confidence in the stock market as an institution. Yet an examination of the latest S.E.C. report on the market, or of its files in innumerable individual investigations, will show you that a great deal of juggling does go on. Personally, I have my doubts that there is any way to stop it. In Wall Street, the caveat of the market place should be translated *Gambler, beware.*

Market rigging did have some effect on my own early experiences in Wall Street.

During my first couple of years in the New York market, I did considerable buying and selling in the American Stock Exchange—Amex. One of the attractions was that Amex—a smaller market than the New York Stock Exchange but nevertheless the nation's second most important—offered a wide range of low-priced stocks.

Like many amateurs in the market, I reasoned: I have only a limited amount of money to invest. Why not get as many shares as I can for it?

It seemed to me that a cheap stock had as good a chance as an expensive one of going up, if not a better chance, since more people would be likely to buy it. And a rise of even a single point on a thousand shares purchased at $10, which did not seem like much of a rise, would be $1,000 profit, whereas a rise of a single point on, say, 100 shares of a $100 stock, for the same investment of $10,000, would hardly be worth mentioning.

As it happens, I was dancing to the wrong music. My reasoning was merely a hangover from my initiation in the Canadian penny market. The fact is that there is a lot more action in the blue chips than the so-called "bargains," at all times. What is more, I made important savings on commissions when I bought and sold the higher-priced stocks. I came to the conclusion that in Wall Street, as elsewhere, it is all too easy to be nickeled to death.

Be this as it may, I did begin to trade in Amex, completely unaware, as thousands of other hopeful small-timers were during this period, that I was bucking a game that could be as crooked as a gaffed roulette wheel.

I was a lot luckier than I deserved to be. I did not, it is true, show any great profit in my over-all operations. But on the other hand I escaped without serious

67

harm, while gambling over a period of a couple of years on a list of stocks that included some real—as it was later proved—ringers.

Among them were the following:

SILVER CREEK PRECISION CORPORATION
THOMPSON-STARRETT CO., INC.
SERVO CORPORATION OF AMERICA
SWAN FINCH OIL CORPORATION

Do any of these ring a bell? The stocks listed above had one thing in common. All were traded by a father-and-son team of Amex specialists named Gerard A. (Jerry) and Gerard F. Re. SWAN FINCH had the additional distinction of being milked by Lowell Birrell a financial genius and master manipulator who is said to have looted more corporations of more millions than any other swindler in the history of the stock market.

Birrell is in Rio.

As for the Res, their activities were, if less spectacular, at the same time far more intimately linked to Amex than Birrell's and probably affected a great many more investors in a far wider range of stocks, none of which could be bought or sold without the consent and participation of the Res.

The SWAN FINCH case, a classic of its kind, is of special interest because it sheds a revealing light on the role of the stock market broker-specialist—the croupier of the Wall Street casino.

I found that the specialist plays an important part in the market.

Commission brokers and their "customers' men," the dealers in the casino, do business directly with the public. As members of a stock exchange, or in association with member-brokers, they are in a position to do for me, as a customer, what I cannot do for myself. That is, buy and sell stocks on the floor of the exchange, a service for which, naturally, they extract the all-important commission.

They do not, however, perform this service single-handed. It is here that the specialist comes in—along with the two-dollar broker, who runs about carrying out the orders of other brokers for a fee, and the odd-lot broker, who buys wholesale and sells piecemeal, through the commission broker, for his own account.

The specialist trades both for his own account and as a service to other brokers. He is called a specialist because he "specializes" in a limited number of stocks, having exclusive privileges where these are concerned. His traditional function as a member of the exchange is to maintain a balanced market in the stocks in which he trades—that means to sell—even from his own account—when there is a demand, and to buy even for his own account when there is an absence of outside buy-orders.

His value to the market in this connection is that he acts as a shock absorber, keeping temporary shortages of a popular stock from driving the price unreasonably high, and, conversely, preventing the sudden and unwarranted drops in price that would result if there were no one to buy a stock when it was offered for sale.

All of this is very important. And naturally, it gives the specialist a great deal of power. Having in his "book" a record of the prices at which various stocks are offered for sale, and another list of prices at which buy-orders have been placed, an unscrupulous specialist is in a position to perform a number of manipulations which will put money into his own pocket.

For example, he will know from his records the price level at which a so-called "stop-loss" sell-order will trigger off other stop-loss orders, and just how low such a series of sales will bring the price of a given stock. Information of this sort is invaluable to a trader who is looking for a killing on a short sale—in which he sells *borrowed* stock at the currently quoted price, and then buys it back to return the borrowed stock when the price comes down. The difference in price is his profit.

The short seller who acts on his own judgment of the price trend is merely gambling on the assumption that the price will come down. But the trader who has had a look at the specialist's "book," and so knows how many sell-orders have been placed, and at what price, is no longer gambling. He is betting on a sure thing. For this reason the specialist is strictly forbidden to show his book to any unauthorized person. And there are a number of other rules governing the transactions he makes for his own account which are designed to keep him from taking unfair advantage of his inside knowledge.

Despite such rules, some specialists have been known to disregard them upon occasion. In fact, studies made by the Securities and Exchange Commission have shown that rigging of the market almost inevitably involves the complicity of a specialist.

In the matter of Re, Re, and Sagarese, as it was referred to in the S.E.C. files, the role ascribed to Jerry Re and his son by the S.E.C. was that of distributor of thousands of shares of unregistered stocks. It was one of the biggest stock-watering operations on record.

Lowell Birrell had acquired, in 1954, 11,682 shares of common stock in the SWAN FINCH COMPANY, or nearly a third of the then outstanding common stock, enough to give him a controlling interest.

SWAN FINCH was important for his purpose. It was an old firm whose shares had long been traded in Amex. Moreover it enjoyed unlisted trading privileges. This meant that, unlike most other corporations, it did not have to file periodic reports required for listed stocks, including statements relating to issuance of new shares.

Birrell busily started an expansion program of *Swan Finch* holdings by a series of corporate acquisitions. These acquisitions were paid for through newly issued SWAN FINCH shares. If the new share had been registered with the Securities and Exchange Commission under the full disclosure of the Securities and Ex-

71

change Act, the public would have been saved a great deal of money.

Shortly after Birrell took control of *Swan Finch,* Jerry Re and his son were designated as specialists in the stock, which had heretofore been handled by another broker-specialist. And, at about the same time, a horse trainer called Charlie Grande opened a brokerage account with the firm of Josephthal & Company.

Almost immediately, the newly issued SWAN FINCH shares, of which there was no public record, began to flow into the market, with the Res as the distributors and Charlie Grande as the nominal seller.

Grande had started out with 5,000 shares of SWAN FINCH. And, as the Securities and Exchange Commission subsequently disclosed, the Res at the same time had acquired 5,000 shares. According to the S.E.C., these transactions were financed by the Penn Fire Insurance Company. Surprise! It turns out that Lowell Birrell was Penn Fire Insurance Company. Birrell finances purchases from Birrell. Whether any money actually changed hands remains in doubt.

At any rate, the 10,000 shares were a drop in the bucket. Thereafter, SWAN FINCH common shares multiplied like fruit flies in summer, and big blocks of the newly issued stock began to move, via horse trainer Charlie Grande and the Res' specialist booth, into the exchange and into the hands of the public.

Within two and a half years, the original SWAN FINCH common, which had consisted of only 35,000 shares, had become 2,016,566 shares. Of this total, from July, 1954, until about April, 1957, the Res distributed no less than 578,000 shares, at market prices totaling more than $3,000,000. Of the total, 481,900 shares, or $1,776,099, moved through Charlie Grande's account. (He later testified that he got out of the market with about $8,000.)

During a single two-month period starting December 18, 1956, Charles Grande was the nominal seller of 441,000 shares of SWAN FINCH, distributed by his friends, the Res. At the same time, other shares were flowing through no fewer than 17 other accounts, which the Securities and Exchange Commission says were dummy accounts controlled by Jerry Re and his son. Most of the shares traded, says the S.E.C., could be traced directly or indirectly to Birrell. None of the shares was ever registered.

The significance of the unlisted trading privileges enjoyed by the SWAN FINCH Company becomes clear at this point, if it wasn't before. Had Birrell been forced to comply with the usual requirements concerning financial reports, the magnitude of his stock-watering operation would have been at once apparent, and would have brought the price down to nothing.

Great pains were taken to support the price.

Charlie Grande's testimony before the Securities and Exchange Commission gives an indication of the method:

Q. Well, you sold 75 shares of the stock (SWAN FINCH) at 16⅞ and then you bought 75 shares at 16⅞, each for the same money.

A. That's right.

Q. Why did you do that?

A. I did a lot of foolish things then.

Q. What reason could you have to make that kind of a transaction?

A. I couldn't give you a reason for it now. I don't even know why I did it, but I did it, and I was having a lot of fun.

While Charlie Grande was having fun, the Res and Birrell were making money. The Res handled sales totaling $3,000,000 in SWAN FINCH, and presumably Birrell got his cut. But the 570,000 shares distributed by the Res account for only a little more than a quarter of the new stock issued. According to the Securities and Exchange Commission, Birrell solved the problem of distributing the remaining shares by the simple process of *pawning* them. They were pledged as security to moneylenders for $1,500,000. When the loans were defaulted, the moneylenders began to dump the shares they held, claiming the privilege of selling the stock without registering it with the Securities and Exchange Commission, on the grounds that these were "distress" sales, and so exempt from registration.

The S.E.C. contested the claim, charging, in effect, that the moneylenders were merely middlemen in an illicit distribution of stock. But it was not until April, 1957, that the American Stock Exchange finally suspended all trading in SWAN FINCH stock. And another year and a half had passed before the Res received so much as a slap on the wrist for their part in the deal. When it came, it was in the form of a 30-day suspension which affected only the elder Re. Matters were so arranged, even then, that the suspension period coincided with Jerry Re's annual January vacation in Florida.

Indictment of the Res did not come until considerably later, after an investigation, reaching from top to bottom of the American Exchange, which revealed that the two specialists were by no means the only members of the Exchange engaged in questionable practices.

Security and Exchange Commission records indicate the participation of a number of floor traders, in complicity with the Res in the manipulation of THOMPSON-STARRETT stock, for the purpose of boosting the offering price of a secondary issue. And similar practices—"painting the tape," in the Wall Street idiom—were disclosed in connection with a dozen other stocks, not in isolated instances but as common practice over a number of years.

The true nature of the sickness afflicting the nation's second largest stock exchange was highlighted in December, 1961, by the resignation under fire of Amex President Edward McCormick.

McCormick, who nine months earlier had described himself as "the tough cop who came to Wall Street," and boasted that Amex was "the best policed stock exchange in the world," quit his $75,000-a-year post after it came to light that:

1. He was involved in numerous direct conflicts of interest involving the purchase of stock for his own account from companies seeking listing privileges with Amex, including stocks recommended by the Res.
2. While in Havana in 1955 as a guest of the convicted stock swindler Alexander Guterma, a Birrell associate (Birrell for some time made his headquarters in Cuba), the Amex president permitted Guterma to pay a $5,000 gambling debt for him.

At the time, Guterma was seeking an Amex listing for a company that he controlled in partnership with two gamblers. The fact that he did not succeed in obtaining the listing did little to save McCormick's reputation for good judgment. Nor did the episode provide any reassurance to a public which was soon to get a fuller report of irregularities in Amex, in an inquiry which proved to be merely a prelude to a full-scale investigation of the entire stock market, backed by a Congressional appropriation of $750,000.

A footnote to the McCormick affair. One evening

before dinner I happened to be having a cocktail in Reuben's, alone, when who should appear at my side but McCormick himself.

I was amazed to hear the president of the American Stock Exchange, red-faced and looking very aggressive, say to me in a loud voice: "I know you! You're the man who says he made two million dollars in the stock market. I hope you realize—" he went on in an even louder voice, "how much harm you've done to the market with that damn book of yours."

For a moment I failed to understand what he was talking about. Then it dawned on me. The wide sale of *How I Made $2,000,000 in the Stock Market* should have pleased the officials of any stock exchange, because it has stimulated new interest in stocks, as any success story relating to the market is bound to do. But there had been an unexpected reaction. As the result of the disclosure of my use of stop-loss orders, a flood of such orders had been placed. The effect had been—not once, but a number of times—to set off a chain reaction of selling when a stock dipped in price, with one stop-loss triggering the next.

The price would go down in rapid-fire order, an eighth of a point or even a quarter on each successive sale, until the accumulation of stop-loss orders on the specialist's "book" had been exhausted. Then, of course, the price would rise again, as traders covering short sales and market bargain hunters would begin to buy.

In a market like Amex, with a volume of trading relatively low in comparison with that of the Big Board, fluctuations so rapid and erratic were not welcomed.

The reason was, of course, that such movements made nonsense of all the brokers' talk about stock "values," and showed the market up for what it was—a casino.

As a direct result of the publication of my book, the officials of Amex had been forced to suspend the use of stop-loss orders—and the suspension remains to this day. (You can still place such orders in the New York Stock Exchange, but even the Big Board will on occasion suspend the practice temporarily, on some particular stock, when too many stop-losses are piling up.)

Clearly I had not made a friend of McCormick. He continued to bluster, and my efforts to calm him down were worse than useless. Finally I had to tell him flatly: "Please, Mr. McCormick, you are making a scene. I came in here for a quiet drink and I'd like to finish it, so go away before I lose my temper."

"The tough cop who came to Wall Street" looked at me in silence for a moment, then turned and walked away. There is one thing to be said for being an acrobatic dancer. It keeps you in shape.

The incident at the bar occurred in October, 1961. Two months later I read about McCormick's resignation and thought to myself: Now who was it he said was "wrecking" the market?

I have not touched on the matters of stock watering and stock rigging merely to moralize about the market. Rigging is almost inevitable in nearly any sort of gambling when the stakes are high enough, and the stock market is essentially a gambling operation with stakes that run into the billions of dollars.

Since the Securities and Exchange Commission has come into being, as an aftermath of the great Wall Street crash of 1929, a number of legal restrictions have been imposed on the brokerage community—always in the face of fierce opposition from Wall Street. Brokerage houses that formerly fought the S.E.C. now regard its presence as good advertising, an assurance to the public of the respectability of gambling on stocks. And although certain practices which were formerly lawful are now illicit, not too much has really changed, as the latest S.E.C. reports clearly show.

Since all it takes is an understanding among traders to make a "pool," and start "dummy" trading, it is virtually undetectable when the "tape is painted" and my belief is that no amount of legislation or policing will end it.

My own conclusion has been that to the investor it really does not make much difference. The truth is, as I was to discover, that—all stock "values" being artificial—there is no *practical* difference between the

79

fluctuations in price produced by manipulation and those which occur naturally as the result of supply and demand. In either case the price change looks the same on the ticker.

Floor traders and serious speculators—and I consider myself one because who can be light about money —protect themselves by judicious use of the "stop-loss" order—an order placed through one's broker with a specialist. It is an order to sell when the price of the stock falls to a predetermined level.

The use of the automatic stop-loss was essential in connection with my discovery—or evolution, if you like—of my "box" theory by which I was to make more than $2,000,000 in the stock market.

At the time I was trading on the American Stock Exchange, I had not yet perfected the box theory. However, I realized already that it was vital to be protected from an unexpected fall in the price of my stocks. And I found that 99 per cent of the time a stop-loss order was an absolute protection against any serious loss; although one cannot be absolutely sure that it will be possible to execute a stop-loss order at precisely the price stipulated. Sometimes the volume of sell-orders is too great and my order is one among many.

Now comes the reason I have devoted the preceding pages to the subject of stock rigging. During the period I traded in American Exchange, I speculated in a number of stocks which, unbeknownst to me, were being manipulated. On the tape they looked like any other stock in upward trend. SWAN FINCH was one of them. I bought it when it was almost at its highest manipulated price, and was sold out automatically a few days later when the price collapsed. My loss—because of the stop-loss order—was negligible.

In the case of THOMPSON-STARRETT, the identical pattern occurred.

Both SWAN FINCH and THOMPSON-STARRETT dropped frighteningly. If I had not evolved certain safeguards, their downward plunge would have meant financial catastrophe for me. The saving factor in each case was the fact that I had learned the importance of the stop-loss order. Through earlier experiences I had learned to use it in order to conserve the major part of my profits. This I did by steadily moving my stop-loss up behind a rising stock.

For example, my records show that in December of 1959 I bought 1,000 shares of BORNE CHEMICAL at 28. It rose steadily to 34, 36, 39, and I posted my stop-losses at 31, then at 32, then at 37 as the uptrend continued.

In January BORNE CHEMICAL reached 39½, then abruptly started to fall. I was automatically sold out at 37. My profit, less buy and sell commissions, came to $8,750.

A broker of my acquaintance told me, about that time, that the stock was being "sponsored" and that I was in on a good thing, provided I was able to get off at the right time. Whether this was actually true or was just one of the innumerable Wall Street rumors to which speculators are constantly exposed, I have no way of knowing. But what is certain is that BORNE CHEMICAL continued on its downward course. At this writing it is selling for about $5\frac{1}{2}$.

Other stocks on which I showed a profit in the American Stock Exchange included:

FAIRCHILD CAMERA

GENERAL DEVELOPMENT

UNIVERSAL CONTROLS

At the time I bought BORNE CHEMICAL, I had reached a point at which a $28,000 investment was by no means remarkable.

Among my holdings at the time were 6,000 shares of UNIVERSAL CONTROLS, bought in 1958, when the firm was known as UNIVERSAL PRODUCTS, at prices ranging from $35\frac{1}{4}$ to 40. Actually, I had bought only 3,000 shares, but soon after I made the purchases there was a 2-for-1 stock split and my shares were doubled. And in March of 1959, the new shares, which had been steadily rising, suddenly went from 66 to 102, and then —just as suddenly—reversed.

Hastily I raised my stop-loss to the last quoted price after the drop had begun and I was sold out immediately, at prices ranging from $86\frac{1}{4}$ to $89\frac{3}{4}$. I was 12 points below the peak, but even so the average selling price was more than twice what I had paid for the stock. Net profit: $409,000.

This was only one of a number of major transactions of that period. Not surprisingly, I took my losses, too. The list of losses included:

AMERICAN MOTORS	$5,844
ADDRESSOGRAPH-MULTIGRAPH	$4,453
AMERICAN METALS-CLIMAX	$7,487

And, in fact, I seemed to be working my way through the alphabet, as the losses piled up, from BRUNSWICK-BALKE-COLLENDER, $5,447, to WARNER-LAMBERT, $3,861.

But at the same time I was getting my master's degree in the fine art of stock market gambling; and, if some of the losses were painful, I was nevertheless paying my way with more than a little something to spare.

The losses listed above—and there were others—came as the result of abandoning, at first from overconfidence and later in despair, the methods by which I had made my first important winnings—the methods which were to make my fortune once I had perfected them.

I cannot say that the market rigging that subsequently produced a scandal in the American Exchange really made any great difference to me, one way or the other. If Amex gradually lost its initial attraction for me, it was because I was no longer looking for the "bargains" that had first drawn me there. I had learned the lesson that bargains in the stock market are invariably expensive. This is no paradox. It is based on simple arithmetic.

The lower the price of the shares I bought, the higher the rate of the commission I paid. The New York Stock Exchange speaks of an "average" commission of 1 per cent, but the fact is that bargain hunters must pay far more. As an extreme example, the broker's commission on a round lot of 100 shares of a $1 stock is $6, a full 6 per cent. If I have $10,000 to invest, and put it all in stock at $1 a share, my total commission will be

$$\$6 \text{ per } 100 \text{ shares} = \$600$$

Assuming for the sake of simplicity that the price remains unchanged and I decide to sell, there will be another commission of $600 to pay. Total: $1,200, or 12 per cent of my capital at one swoop. Plus tax. How long can I play in the Big Casino at that rate?

On the other hand, let us assume that I take the same $10,000 and buy 100 shares of the highest-priced stock I can afford at $100 per share. The commission on buying the stock will be only $49 when I buy, another $49 when I sell. Total: $98. Quite a difference, is there not?

These commission figures illustrate a point I learned (all other factors being equal)—*I buy the most expensive stock I can afford and I buy it in round lots.*

I went through all the common temptations. How

about the low-priced growth stocks the brokers were always talking about? And what about those quality stocks that had fallen in price during a temporary drop in the market, but were certain to make a comeback when the market improved?

Someone is always ready to tell me how rich I would be if I had bought GENERAL MOTORS 30 years ago, when it was selling for $5 per share, and stayed with it through stock splits which would have given me, by now, six shares for every one, currently selling at about $81.

Very good growth indeed, assuming that I had a reasonable amount of money to invest 30 years ago, and could afford to wait it out. But I counter the GENERAL MOTORS example, with, "Well, sure, but how about NEW YORK CENTRAL, which hit $259 per share in 1929 and now, after 34 years, is selling at 21-7/8, with NO stock splits.

The truth is that my chart books are filled with stocks that have never recovered to anything approaching their all-time highs; and for every old-timer that is making a big splash today, there are two others that have gone out of business completely. Occasionally, an old movie star makes a comeback. It is an occasion indeed. Meanwhile, how many are in homes for aged and itinerant actors?

My recollections of growth stocks are no better. Remember the uranium boom of the early 1950's? Some 500 companies with uranium exploration leases and

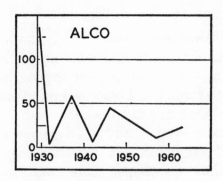

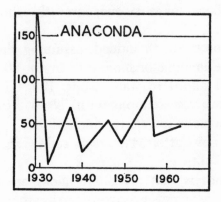

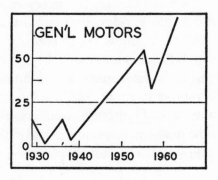

futuristic names have gone out of business since then. The stocks of all of them were bargains at the time. Very low-priced.

So are toy balloons—cheap and very attractive. But they have a tendency to burst.

By the same token, I found that not *all* high-priced stock are good buys. My experience tells me it is foolish to buy a stock or anything else on the basis of price alone. NEW YORK CENTRAL was once a blue chip and so were many others now in their old age and acting anything but chipper. Just some examples:

ALCO PRODUCTS hit 136 in 1929, was selling for 59 in 1937, and currently is around 23, still waiting for a comeback.

ANACONDA COPPER reached an all-time high of 175 in 1929; it is now $52\frac{1}{2}$.

BURROUGHS CORPORATION was once 113; today it's around 23.

U.S. SMELTING was once 131. This year it took a sharp upward spurt but where is 131?

The comeback trail can be a long, weary road. Many a stock that backslides never can make it up the hill again.

So-called growth stocks do come along occasionally, and big killings are made on them when they do, as I myself have reason to know. But what has become of the glamor stocks of yesterday—stocks like TECHNICOLOR that were all the rage before color film became a standardized part of the movie industry?

In the late 1950's, the boom in space issues, so-called, produced some wonderful windfalls, for those who got in at the right time—and got out at the right time. One of my most spectacular breaks was in a then little-known stock named THIOKOL.

I made my first really large purchase of 1,300 shares early in 1958 at 49⅞, took a profit, used the money to buy rights in more THIOKOL, and subsequently, through the maximum use of credit and the good fortune of a 3-for-1 split, wound up with a total profit of $862,000.

That is what you call growth! However, I should say here that I did not buy THIOKOL when it was one among many cheap stocks. If so, I could have had it at 19; but by this time I was wary of false bargains. I had my own box system well worked out, and THIOKOL didn't even begin to interest me until it had passed 45 and looked as though it would go over 50. It did, and the rise which followed, continuing after the split, carried it all the way to 72 before it began to back down again.

Timing was the important thing, and had nothing to do with fundamentals or even with "growth" as such; *it had to do with the behavior of the stock on the market!*

I got out—after a 3-for-1 split—at 68, fantastically far ahead of the game. A friend of mine made the mistake of getting *in* just about this time, following the late-coming crowd. He bought at 65. Today he is still "locked in," with several thousand dollars of his money tied up—and the price is currently around 19.

The THIOKOL enterprise itself is still growing; it recently received an important government rocket contract, and the dividend is now $1.10 per share, all of which greatly encourages my friend. His broker tells him that the stock is obviously "worth" much more than its market price, and so is bound to rise. Will it?

My experiences warn me that the price of a stock really has nothing to do with its earnings (except when a sufficient number of buyers happen to *think* it does, and act on their belief).

It is anticipation of growth rather than growth itself that makes for lively speculation and big profits in the so-called growth stocks.

The stock market axiom is "Buy cheap, sell dear." I make my own rule; I buy when the ticker shows that the price is going UP, and I never regret it—whether I buy cheap or dear. And it won't matter whether the croupier is gaffing the wheel or not.

CHAPTER FOUR

The Touts

I HAVE A BROKER in New York—one of several, and there is no need to name them here—whose greatest virtue is that he is entirely without imagination. In his profession he doesn't need it. His function is merely to sit in the middle and cut the pot; and for that, imagination is unnecessary. It might even be a handicap.

From my point of view he is ideal; because he is absolutely honest, doesn't gossip, and does exactly what I ask. When I say buy, he buys. When I say sell, he sells. When I ask the price of a stock—he knows the answer. It pays him to know, because I am a good customer. Sometimes his commissions on my transactions have run as high as $8,000 a month.

But I have sometimes wondered what can go on in that man's head. He has been handling a part of my account for years. He knows how I operate. He has seen me make as much as $80,000 in a single day. And still he doesn't believe what I tell him.

My ideas mean nothing to him. He is sure there must be a trick to it somewhere because, from his point of view, it is all wrong. He lives by the Rothschild rule, "Buy cheap, sell dear." I am sure, although I have never been in this broker's office in all the years of our association, that he must have that motto framed on the wall above his desk.

It is like him: He is sure I must be mad; because I do exactly the opposite of what the motto decrees—I buy stocks when they are dear, and sell as soon as they show signs of becoming cheap.

It never seems to occur to Mr. X—let's call him that—that I may be right. He is convinced I *can't* be right, even though he has seen me make a fortune—because my methods contravene the articles of faith of his religion. Wall Street to him is not a casino but a church, and he is a true believer. He believes in "fundamentals," in stocks as an investment, in the mumbo-jumbo about "shares in American business."

And the truth is that many, perhaps most, stockbrokers are the same. They see how the market behaves, but they gain no insight from their observation. They are too imbued with the cant of their profession to see it as it is.

Of course, they are not to be blamed. In the first place, their living depends on keeping the casino going, and they know by instinct or by reason that the come-on of the carnival barker won't do the trick. People want to be assured that they are buying something more than lottery tickets when they buy stocks, and brokers must find or invent plausible reasons for switching their customers from one lottery ticket to another—if they are going to keep the commissions coming in.

In the second place, they themselves are snowed under by the avalanche of advice, explanations, rationalization, prophecy, and propaganda manufactured by an army of touts who live, like industrious sparrows, on the rich pickings to be found in Wall Street.

If my Mr. X is a true believer in the Wall Street temple—and he is—these people are the high priests, the medicine men, the snake-oil pitchmen of the financial community. They range from the $100,000-a-year market analyst—member of an exclusive and aristocratic little club of Wall Street consultants—to the $150-a-week brokerage house copywriter, who advises millionaires but has his lunch at the Automat; on down to the shameless market tipster who hustles his green or pink sheet of "hot issues," "mystery stocks," and so on for anything from a dollar a week to three or four hundred dollars a year.

Stockbrokers like to think of themselves as members of a dignified—and even learned—profession; and most of the advertising copy churned out by Madison Avenue on their behalf is designed to build up this image.

Judging from the advertising, the typical stockbroker is a sort of financial Dr. Kildare—interested, kindly, knowledgeable, ready at all times to take your economic pulse and to prescribe for your ailing fortune and anemic pocketbook.

That a profession charged with grave social and economic responsibilities should advertise at all gives the game away. Imagine how it would be if the medical profession were to follow the same practice!

"Carbuncles removed painlessly at low cost! Is your blood pressure too low? Try our rapid blood-building program. Modern techniques and latest equipment at your service. Special bargain in amputations, this week only! Appendectomies are cheaper than ever! Free antibiotics with every treatment!"

Ridiculous, and a bit shocking, yes. But if stock brokerage should be taken seriously, as a social service and not merely an accessory to the gambling house, then what is the difference between an ad which says "Have you had your liver checked recently?" and one which invites you to "Write for a free analysis of your investment portfolio?"

The difference, of course, is that you don't gamble with your health, if you can help it. You *do* gamble with your money, and that is what "investment" in stocks is. The pity is that the people who give advice in the casino don't usually know very much about gambling. *Their* business is collecting commissions. Or, on the tip-service level, reading tea leaves for a fee.

In one instance which came to my attention not long ago, it turned out that an advisory service purporting to cover "all facets of finance" in a weekly market letter, was conducting its entire service from a Fifth Avenue mail drop. The actual premises of the service which claimed to review the entire world of finance in all its ramifications were the director's living room where his girl friend industriously cranked a mimeograph machine and licked stamps.

The man who ran the service could not afford to pay office rent. His business was in his hat. If his market forecasts had been worth anything, he surely would have been acting on them himself, not selling them at $2 for a six-week trial subscription.

The case is not uncommon. The first market tipster was the serpent in the Garden of Eden, and his advice on apple futures seems to have set the pattern for succeeding generations, unto the present day.

Happily for the hucksters, people will buy almost anything that is represented as a bargain, even if it is worthless, and I must admit that, at one time or another, I have taken trial subscriptions for almost every service I have seen advertised.

Most of them talked a great game, but when I came to analyze what they were telling me, I found that it was impossible to get concrete information. "Buy on reaction." Fine, but when does the reaction start? How much shall I pay? When shall I sell? Often recommendations for "growth stocks," "stocks for quick profits," and the like were diametrically opposed. What one service liked, another put down. And then there was a forecasting service which offered a consensus of other forecasters—much like the "Consensus" column in the *Morning Telegraph* racing form.

Some of my purchases were nothing short of disastrous—or would have been if I had stuck with the advice of the tipsters. For instance, there was EMERSON RADIO, strongly touted by a company which virtually proved, with charts, graphs, and abstruse technical analysis, that—although the stock was selling for around $12—it was easily "worth" $30 or more. I bought it at the "bargain" price of 12½, but was wise enough or lucky enough to cash in my chips when it started down. By the end of the year it was at 5¾. That was in 1956. In 1963 it was around 9. I shouldn't be surprised if I were told today, by one service or another, that it has everything going for it and is sure to rise. I don't doubt that it may, some day. But when? And how long must I keep my money tied up in it while awaiting the great day?

While performing in Tokyo in 1957, I received from my broker three consecutive weekly market letters of a well-known advisory service—all strongly urging subscribers to dump LORILLARD, in which I then had a big investment. I had bought much of it at 35 and 36½. It was at 44 when the advisory service recommended that it be sold. When I finally did sell, it was at an average of 57⅜ and I made a profit of more than $21,000.

If I had paid any attention to the crystal ball gazers in New York, I'd have reduced that profit by about $17,000. Fortunately, by then the box theory was in operation and I had no intention of selling until the stock stopped making money for me.

The market forecasters have their own way of making money, and you can bet that in most instances it is definitely *not* by taking their own advice. That's for the gambling public, which has made tips on the market at so much a week or so much a year a multi-million-dollar industry.

Some services, it is only fair to say, do attempt to provide fair value, and succeed, to the extent that they give their customers the *technical tools* with which to observe the market, by charting the performance of individual stocks, making cost and earnings comparisons, and so on. But tip services with their own axes to grind are not unheard of, by any means.

A case in point is that of a veteran market analyst named Frank Payson Todd, who published investment advice under the title of "The New England Counsellor."

In 1955, about the time I was getting a foot in the door in Wall Street, Todd was engaged, for a fee of $500, to evaluate the financial program of CANADIAN JAVELIN.

Shortly thereafter Todd became a stockholder in the company, with 17,000 shares which he bought from CANADIAN JAVELIN officials for $70,500 of *their* money. The purchase price was covered, according to the records of the Securities and Exchange Commission, by unsecured loans to Todd. Whether any cash actually changed hands is not known. In any case, Todd got the stock. The company officials received his IOU's.

No sooner had Todd become a CANADIAN JAVELIN shareholder than his hundreds of newsletter subscribers began to hear marvelous things about the stock of CANADIAN JAVELIN from "The New England Counsellor."

When the postal service proved too slow to keep up with the urgency of the investment situation, as Todd saw it in relation to his (by now) favorite stock, he sent out special reports on CANADIAN JAVELIN by telegram. According to the S.E.C., a JAVELIN official shelled out $3,700 to help pay for these messages of glad tidings and great joy.

CANADIAN JAVELIN, which boomed for a short while on the strength of the reports, is still traded on the Amex board. But its chief sponsor, Todd, has been put out of the tipster business, his S.E.C. registration revoked in 1960 for gross violations of the investment advisers' code of ethics.

The code, and the S.E.C., provide some protection against collusion, but can do little to protect the public from itself—when it is blinded by the lure of quick and easy money.

Slick stock salesmen have found that there is literally nothing that can't be sold to someone, and no claim is too outlandish for those who wish to believe. In an age of scientific miracles, everything is miraculous. Why not flying saucers? Why not excursions to the moon? From 1958 through 1960, investors in the state of New York actually put more than $50,000 into stock in O.T.C. ENTERPRISES, the brain child of a con man named Otis T. Carr, on his assurance that the company had developed a space ship—in effect a flying saucer—that could and would take favored stockholders to the moon.

As if that were not enough, Carr further claimed that the engine which was to propel his flying saucer could run indefinitely without fuel; in effect, perpetual motion!

At last report Carr was serving time in Oklahoma for stock fraud, but it is interesting to note that, although he went to jail in Oklahoma, not one of the citizens he fleeced was offered any hope of getting his money back.

A survey conducted by the New York Stock Exchange in 1959 disclosed that fully 40 per cent of the Americans who owned stock at that time could not say precisely what a common stock was. They owned one or more shares of the stuff. They had paid money for it, and hoped to make money on it. But—what was it?

Of the 12,800,000 persons who were then considered to be "on the verge" of buying shares, the New York Stock Exchange discovered, half could not give an adequate definition of a share of common stock. Would they consider investing in common stock? Sure. Judging by all they had heard, 6,500,000 Americans thought it might be a good idea. What was it they were considering, exactly? None could say with any certainty, except that it related to that avenue paved with solid gold bricks, Wall Street.

No wonder the tipsters rake in the hay!

The first reference to market forecasting that I have been able to find, in checking back over the history of Wall Street, was in connection with an advertisement in the *New York Times* in 1898, by the firm of Haight & Freese, bankers and commission stockbrokers.

Then as now the lure was profits!

> *The best of reasons exist for believing that we will have a January rise. . . .*

And there was an attractive offer of something for nothing!

> *Write or call for our "400-Page Manual," illustrated with railroad maps, giving complete*

*location of all Railroad and Industrial proper-
ties, including highest and lowest prices for a
series of 10 to 30 years of Stocks, Bonds, Grain,
and Cotton, and also methods of buying and
selling on margin.*

In Wall Street, there are always "the best of reasons"
for anticipating a rise. In this respect, nothing has
really changed since 1898, except the language of the
sales pitch, which is more insistent and somewhat more
pretentious than formerly.

HUGE PROFIT POTENTIAL!

ONE STOCK NEARLY EVERY INVESTOR
SHOULD HAVE!

VALUE SELECTIONS!

12 DIFFERENT WAYS TO SEEK INVEST-
MENT SUCCESS!

WE ARE NOW IN A BULL MARKET!

Almost without exception, the tip services and tea
leaf readers have one commodity for sale: like the race
track tout, they claim to know the names of the winners, and will let you in on the secret—for a modest

fee. In the Wall Street tout sheets, it never rains, the weather is always fair, the market is always a bull market, or on the point of becoming one.

STOCKS FOR GROWTH! SPECIAL SITUATIONS IN A "SLEEPING GIANT" INDUSTRY! EXTRAORDINARY REWARDS!

Why don't the tipsters get in on this growth, put a little money on the sleeping giants, and rake in the extraordinary rewards themselves? They manage to sound like philanthropists, but it is obvious that, if they must sell their special information to others, it is because it is not special enough to do anything with themselves.

Prophecy! It's wonderful. But I found that I could save a lot of money by looking at the daily newspaper, in which I quickly discovered my own sleeping giants through observing how the stocks *performed* and which are actually performing best.

Recently I received a letter from one of the better-known market-prediction services inquiring:

> Dear Friend:
>
> Have you ever wished that you could have your own private electronic "brain" to help you in your stock selections? Just think—you

could feed information into it and—in seconds
—out would come answers vitally important in
making market projections. . . .

Some time ago we posed a special problem
for our computer "brain." We wanted to find
out which issues were the best growth possi-
bilities for the next buying opportunity. . . . So
we fed a wealth of data into the machine. And
the machine gave us the answers!

The crystal-ball-gazing industry has now gone electronic. For only $37.50 for a regular seven month sub-
scription, I can get a list of all electronically selected
growth stocks, which I am assured are the "cream" of
long-term capital appreciation issues; stocks that will
go "up and up and up."

Fortunately, I haven't needed an electronic brain to
see which stocks are going "up and up and up." The
newspaper stock tables tell me when a stock actually
is going up, and until then I'm not interested.

Nor do I need electronics to tell me what common
sense tells me: that if science would give the prophets
any such information on market winners, they would
not be selling it for "little more than $1 a week."
They'd keep it to themselves.

A further attraction offered by the forecasting firm
with the electronic brain is a warning service which
purportedly has been saving investors big sums ever

since 1929, by issuing warning bulletins (by mail) whenever the market has been about to collapse.

This may be fine for people who have some stocks in a safe deposit box in the bank that they look at twice a year. But as far as I can see, it is neither as quick nor as efficient as the simple stop-loss order. The electronic brain people will let me know, by mail, when *stocks in general* seem to be slumping. The stop-loss order will tell me nothing, by mail or otherwise. But it does act automatically the moment my *particular stock* starts to lose ground. And it doesn't cost me a dollar a week. It costs me nothing!

How successful are the forecasters of Wall Street, as a group?

They know a bit more about the market, usually, than the Wall Street amateur. That is, they have mastered the *vocabulary* of stocks better, the abracadabra of indexes, trends, averages, options, puts, calls, straddles, spreads, strips, and straps. They know the Dow Line, the profit line, the value line, the odd-lot index. the advance-decline line. But, alas! they have no pipe line to the information that counts: when does *my* stock start going *up*, and how far?

When it comes to telling me the essential information, whether a stock will go UP in price or DOWN in price, the truth is that *blind chance* will produce market predictions about as accurate as any that money can buy.

If I would flip a coin, choose a name that sounds good, try the ink-blot test or the blindfold and straight pin method, the law of averages would give me results about as rewarding as those derived from tipsters and trend prognosticators.

Every day several hundred issues *rise* on the market. Several hundred other issues decline in price. And usually a few score are unchanged for the day, because there is little or no trading in them.

In a strong bull market, I know more stocks will be rising than declining. In a bear market, it will be the other way around. But I don't forget that in either sort of market, there will be movement in *both* directions. And what is more, many of the issues that improved yesterday will sag today. There is no clearcut or permanent division between the UP stocks and the DOWN stocks. If there were, there would be no market, because the DOWNS would soon be wallpaper, and the UPS would price themselves out of circulation.

There is no sure-fire method of knowing which escalator my stock will be on. UP or DOWN? Again, if the touts of Wall Street knew, you can bet they would not be peddling the advice to me—they would be *acting* on it.

Here is a report on the ups and downs of prices on the New York Stock Exchange over an arbitrarily chosen 10-day period, two full trading weeks:

104

	Advances	Declines	Unchanged	Total Number Issues Traded
Jan. 14	723	360	249	1,332
Jan. 15	504	556	255	1,315
Jan. 16	337	720	246	1,303
Jan. 17	712	333	259	1,304
Jan. 18	572	509	238	1,319
Jan. 21	567	485	266	1,318
Jan. 22	672	390	249	1,311
Jan. 23	619	428	264	1,311
Jan. 24	571	464	251	1,286
Jan. 25	588	461	240	1,289

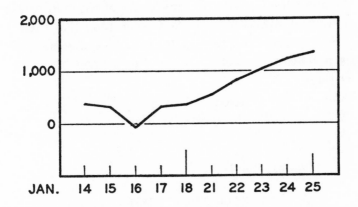

Add up the gains and losses of the first week, day by day, and you will see it was not such a good week, from the *trend* dopester's point of view. On Monday,

105

the 14th, twice as many stocks went up in price as declined, and market writers cried, "Hurray! things are looking better than ever." On Wednesday, the 16th, the trend was almost exactly reversed. Groans in Wall Street. On Thursday, the 17th, the pendulum swings back again, lots of winners, less than half as many losers. On Friday, the 18th, there is little to choose between one group and the other.

The second week was all in favor of the winners, although there was a substantial number of losers, too. However, if I had been adding the plus and minus factors on a daily basis, as the so-called Advance-Decline Line chartists do, my chart of the two weeks of trading would have looked something like this:

By January 25, I would have been quite cheerful. As a matter of fact, so were the market reporters, writing:

> MARKET RISES
> IN UPHILL PULL

and two days later:

> MARKET CLIMBS
> TO HIGH FOR '63

Wonderful! That is, fine for the tipsters, who had been predicting great things all along, and now had a better than 50/50 chance to be right in their fore-

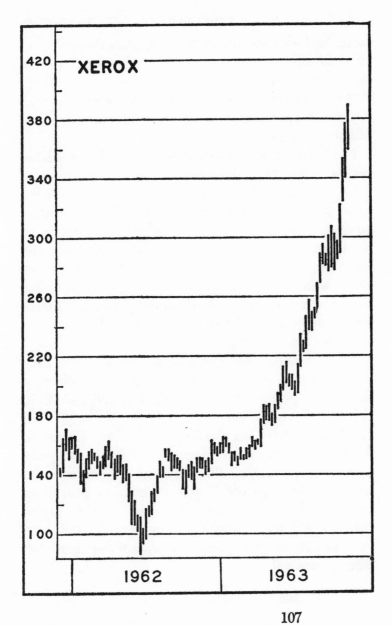

XEROX

casts. And all very interesting to market theorists and chart keepers—especially to those who did *not* have their money invested.

But suppose my "mystery stock," or "sleeping giant," or "No. 1 speculative issue" did not happen to be following the zigs and zags of the chart?

Don't forget that every single day of the 10-day period, while several hundred stocks were rising in price, several hundred others—*and not always the same ones*—were going down. The individual issues were by no means multiple yo-yos on a collective string. Some went down with the general decline, following the chart line. And then on days when the majority of stocks were rising, they *continued* to go down. A few even sank to record new lows. And, by the same token, quite a few hit new *highs,* on days when the chart line indicated a general dip.

I compare the graphs of individual stocks over long periods of time with the charts which supposedly map the over-all performance of the market, and I see that, although there is a general correlation, the more than 1,300 issues listed on the New York Stock Exchange do not necessarily move in unison. They are sheeplike in some respects, yes. But they are not sheep. Some issues, in fact, go completely counter to prevailing trends. Many seem to act with no relationship to the trends at all—for months or years on end. Their personalities are contrary. *Buy, and they slump. Sell, and they bounce up!*

Mystery stocks is right! And the evidence indicates that the men who make a living predicting what they will do are no better at it than the gambling public. At the very least, you would expect them to do as well as if they used the blindfold and straight pin. As an actor in a play once said, "Even a clock that has stopped is right twice every twenty-four hours."

Simple logic tells me that in any market in which more stocks are *rising* in price than are declining—and that means, of course, a bullish market—the law of averages will give me more winners, no matter what method I use to select stocks.

I can hang the *Wall Street Journal* on a door and fling darts at it, as a famous cosmetologist is reputed to have done. Or I can put on a blindfold and stab at the stock chart with my finger. If more stocks are going up than are going down, I will have to be fantastically unlucky not to hit more winners than losers.

I personally know a prosperous Manhattan attorney who has made substantial sums by just such a method. He spreads out the *Barron's* stock chart for the week on his desk, closes his eyes, and sticks a pin in the paper. Where it sticks, he buys.

Sure, he has lost money on some stocks. But in a strong market he has won even more.

Considering the foregoing, it is not surprising that the Wall Street tipsters occasionally come up with good selections, especially during boom periods, when a lot of new money is coming into the Wall Street casino and more stocks are rising than declining. If only by the simple law of averages, the forecasters should be able to do at least as well as my friend, the attorney, who chooses stocks with his eyes shut.

Do they? Here is where I was in for a surprise. *The forecasters don't make as good a showing in the stock market as they could by the simple law of averages.*

A study undertaken by the Cowles Commission for Economic Research in 1933 revealed that the predictions of the nation's leading forecasters, flooding the country with thousands of "authoritative" news letters on market trends, Dow Lines, advance-decline lines, value lines, etc., *hit the mark with 4 per cent LESS accuracy than if their selections had been made absolutely at random.*

The Cowles Commission survey was repeated in 1944, with virtually the same results.

Pure chance—throwing darts at the *Wall Street Journal* or sticking pins in *Barron's*—would have given the prophets even odds, or 50 per cent accuracy. In other words, they would have been right at least *half the time.* They were not. Their collective score in two successive surveys was *only 46 per cent.*

Needless to say, their poor showing has not discouraged the crystal-ball-gazers. Why should it? They don't gamble. They *advise* the gamblers—for a fee. Gamblers come and go broke, but the well-established

110

forecasting service continues to prosper—year in, year out.

It is no exaggeration to say that the advice of some self-styled market analysts is on a par with what is in Rajah Rahbo's *Dream Book*. Strange as it may seem in a supposedly hard-headed business world, many stockbrokers themselves are passionate numerologists. They have given up trying to make sense of the market in the usual ways, and spend their off hours looking for lucky numbers or—in an equally popular related field—guidance from the stars.

I have heard of at least one professional investment adviser in Wall Street who actually bases his predictions on astrology. And the funny thing is that, as far as I can tell, it works about as well as the electronic brain—because the truth is that neither stars nor machines can tell what the gamblers in Wall Street are going to do, until they are actually doing it. And then, of course, the price quotations on the ticker can tell me, better than any other device yet invented, what stocks are doing.

I FOUND THAT THE BEST PLACE TO LOOK FOR THE TIP-OFF TO THE MARKET IS IN THE MARKET.

But of course many market forecasters don't go to the trouble to chart the course of the market. Like race track touts, they need tips to peddle *every day*—and the market itself is not always sufficiently generous for their business requirements. Like touts they work on a simpler system: promote as many horses as possible in every race, and some of them are sure to come in.

The same system can be applied to selection in any field. Every so often someone finds a hidden fortune in an old mattress, or buried in the cellar, or thrown down a well. If tomorrow I decide to establish a Fortune Finding Service, and advertise:

> *This week look in your cellar . . .*
> *Also recommended are attics . . .*
> *Haystacks . . .*
> *Between the leaves of books published before 1905 . . .*

it is virtually certain that some of my clients will find some money.

Then next week I can advertise:

> *Mrs. L. D. of Omaha, Neb., taking our advice of Aug. 15, found $400 in her cellar. J. B. of Mongoose, Wisc., found $160 in gold double eagles in a trunk in his attic. . . .*

It would be easy enough to explain, in technical language the "system" for determining that cellars are better places to find money than, for example, corner newsstands or public bathing beaches. If I wanted to dress up the method with some charts and graphs, that would be easy, too.

112

SOURCES OF TREASURE

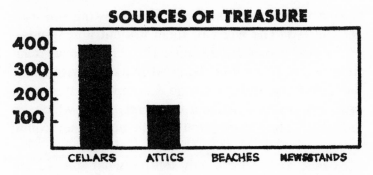

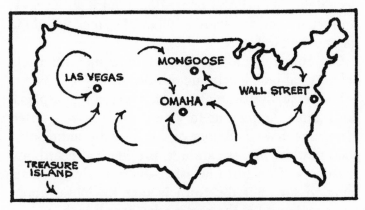

Geographical Centers of Treasure-Finding Activity
in the United States Last Week

Obvious nonsense, isn't it? Yet when it is translated into the special language of Wall Street, it passes for wisdom, and people pay cash money for it.

Why doesn't the public catch on? Probably it does, but the gambling instinct is strong, and there is a constantly replenished public, made up of those who have not yet been burned.

There are numerous schools of forecasting and market analysis. The worst of them are outright frauds— or, in rare instances, the reflection of personal delusions, as in the case of the aged market adviser who, the Securities and Exchange Commission disclosed, drew his predictions from a "secret code" which he thought he had discovered in the newspaper comic strips.

At best, analysis can only tell me what stocks have been doing in the PAST or are doing in the PRESENT. And what I need to know is what MY stock will do in the immediate future.

Unfortunately, no one has yet come up with a reliable crystal ball, electronic or otherwise.

Market analysis can always discover ample explanations, *after the fact*, as to why a given issue spurted upward or fell off. Rumor of a stock split, anticipated good news of higher earnings, presidential heartburn, or rumors of a Cuban invasion—there is always something to say. But the truth is that the observations made at the end of the trading day are all in the nature of post mortems. And they are mostly rationalization in any case.

The truth is that the market behaves as IT does because the gamblers behave as THEY do, and no one can know what they will do until they have done it.

CHAPTER FIVE

Personal Protection: Hedging My Bets

"**G**AMBLING AGAINST the world for life or death," wrote Carlyle. The line reminds me of one or two Wall Street speculators I have met—men who had plunged into the Big Casino over their heads and were desperately risking everything they owned, trying to get out again.

For such temperaments, the warning that a certain risk attaches to all stocks needs to be triply underscored. If stocks were not a gamble, there would be no pay-off. In fact, there would be no market as we know it. Stocks would be sold over the counter like potatoes or government bonds, at fixed prices.

But the reckless, passionate gambler probably is not really typical of the stock market. The more usual atti-

115

tude which characterizes the amateur in the Wall Street casino is a kind of passivity more appropriate to religion than to business.

The average small investor approaches his stock-broker with the hopeful but worried look of a little girl entering a doll hospital. He inquires respectfully as to "good buys" in stocks, listens while the Great Man pontificates—and then hands over his savings and waits for mysterious wheels to turn and render him a profit.

If the profit fails to materialize, the client may conclude that he has been sold a gold-plated brick, but usually he will accept the bad news fatalistically. Stockbrokers, thanks to slick institutional advertising and their priestly function in the temple of Mammon, enjoy a prestige equal to that of physicians. I have yet to meet a man who fails to assure me that *his* doctor is the best doctor in the world.

Brokers inspire the same respect among the true believers in the temple.

"Hmmmm," says the stockbroker, tapping an anemic balance sheet with a well-manicured nail and looking thoughtful. "Just as I thought. A slight technical correction. Nothing to worry about, but suppose, if you're really worried, we switch to, ah—"

And the client goes away with another clinker, instead of the one he has just sold at a loss, and the stockbroker pockets not one but *two* commissions.

It is surprising what a beating some investors can

116

take, and still retain their faith in a market which remains as loftily mysterious to them as it was the day
they entered it. I know a prosperous professional man,
a house physician employed by a chain of luxury ho-
tels, who put his entire life's savings in stocks at the
peak of the big bull market in 1961.

His total investment was some $300,000. The mar-
ket was long overdue for what the brokers like to call
"an adjustment"—although few of them said so except
as a matter of hindsight. And sure enough, in 1962 the
big slump wiped out about two-thirds of my friend
Dr. Y's savings at one blow.

"Well," he told me one day after the dust had set-
tled a bit, when I met him by chance in the lobby of
the Plaza in New York, "after all, I only lost $200,000."
Only $200,000!

Here was a man who had personally earned all that
he owned, a person who would certainly think twice
before making a long distance telephone call to Paris
or telling a cab driver to keep the change from a $5
bill, but he could refer to the bulk of his life's savings
as *only* $200,000.

This is the same sort of passive fatalism—the lack of
a sense of reality with regard to the magic numbers on
the ticker tape—which marks the compulsive gambler
in Las Vegas or Monte Carlo, the man who thinks
nothing of flinging a $5 chip to the boy who brings
him a pack of cigarettes, but would be highly indig-
nant if, under normal circumstances, a shopkeeper

117

were to try to run up the price by even a few cents on those same cigarettes.

Another friend of mine has delusions regarding the outlook for a "comeback" of his depreciated stock. He tells me: "I'm just a little fellow. I can't afford to take an 8-point loss. How can I sell my stock until it comes back to the price at which I bought it?"

My reply: "How can you afford *not* to sell it? Here is a stock that formerly sold at 33, the price you paid for it. It is now selling at 25. If you look at its chart for the past six months or so, you see nothing encouraging about it. It has been on a slow downward trend all along. If you were starting fresh in the market at this moment, you would scarcely select a $25 stock which was formerly much higher and has been doing nothing but losing for months. You'd look for a stock that had been cheaper and was steadily improving. So why don't you get rid of your loser and find yourself a winner?

"Sell now and cut your loss. Or, if you insist on taking further losses and meanwhile keeping your money tied up, figure out the box of your stock, establish the bottom, and set a stop-loss order there. Because if it goes through the bottom of the box, as it seems sure to do, you will have, not a $25 stock, but an $18 or a $15 stock—and who knows how low it will go eventually?"

My experience tells me it is imperative to be realistic about prices. A stock which is selling at 25 is a $25 stock, no matter what I originally paid for it. And so I must appraise it as a $25 stock.

Past and future are words that mean nothing in the stock market, because they are nonexistent. What exists is NOW. Every new day, and every hour of the trading day, brings the demand for new decisions. I never act in the past, nor in the future. I act *now*. And thus a decision to *retain* a losing stock is exactly the same as a decision to *buy* a loser. The same logic obviously applies in reverse to the decision to sell a rising stock. Who goes into the market to *buy* losses and *sell* profits? What an odd philanthropy that would be! And yet people do it every day.

They do it through ignorance, through timidity, and because they believe in myths and magical solutions to their problems, rather than rational ones. They *feel* when they should be *thinking*.

The Plaza's captain in the Oak Room, Victor, with whom I am on friendly terms, bought 100 shares of CHRYSLER in 1962 for $42 (before the 2-for-1 split), watched it rise slowly to $72, and then sold—for what he considered a very nice profit of $3,000.

He seemed mildly surprised when I asked him *why* he had sold. "Why?" he said. "Well, why *not*? I'm way ahead of the game, and, anyway, I didn't want to get too greedy. I'm satisfied."

His answer indicates nothing more nor less than pure superstition before the mysteries of the great money market. Don't get greedy, or the gods will be angry, and snatch back what they have given.

I told my friend that, if he was satisfied, that was all that mattered. But it could not have been much consolation later, because the fact is that CHRYSLER, far from having reached its peak, was just beginning a spectacular run that was to take it all the way up to 108, before a 2-for-1 split.

Nor was that the end of the run. The 1963 CHRYSLER high for the new shares, at this writing, is 89¼. The equivalent price in the pre-split shares would have been 178½. In other words, the man who didn't want to be greedy sold out just before a rise that would have *doubled* his money within a few months!

The curious combination of passivity and mysticism that characterizes many "investors" in the stock market may be the key to the success of various types of collectives operating in the market.

Since most small bettors don't trust their own judgment, they tend to seek safety in numbers. And since they don't like the day-to-day responsibility of deciding what to do in the market, they seek someone wise in the ways of the financial world to do their thinking for them. The trouble is that this *someone* is invariably a pro, who must consider *his* profit first and last, if he is to pay the rent on his shiny office and keep well stocked in bourbon and good cigars.

There are various folds in which the sheep seek safety and guidance. Since sheep shearing is the ordained occupation of shepherds, it stands to reason that the safety-in-numbers believers are almost certain to get clipped, coming and going.

Investment Clubs

I looked into investment clubs and I found that there are an estimated 25,000 of them in the United States. Some of them are informal little groups organized along the lines of afternoon dessert-bridge clubs, whose members may well be more interested in the fudge cake and peach ice cream than the business of plotting stock trends. But thousands are sufficiently large and active to have their own accountant, attorneys, and bonded treasurer.

The investment club usually attracts the sort of investor who would like to make a little money in the stock market, but doesn't want to go overboard, or can't afford to invest enough in a single lump sum to avoid the excessive commissions and odd-lot charges that relate to buying a few shares of stock at a time.

The National Association of Investment Clubs, which provides professional guidance in the establishment of such organizations, at $1 per member per annum, sets "appreciation," meaning increased market value of stocks purchased, as the primary goal of investment, and lays it down as a basic rule that all dividends be reinvested rather than shared among the members.

121

How do the clubs fare? According to a 1960 National Association of Investment Clubs survey, the *average* gain in holdings of clubs which followed N.A.I.C. rules by investing only in growth stocks and reinvesting all dividends, was 8 per cent; in clubs established more than five years, the growth rate was said to be 11 per cent on the average.

However, this is to speak of clubs rather than individual members, who come and go. The average club, in or out of the National Association of Investment Clubs, generally loses rather than gains during the first year or two of its existence, owing partly to the fact that the rate of investment is low and the commissions are high—usually around 6 per cent.

And as John W. Hazard and Lew C. Colt point out in *The Kiplinger Book on Investing for the Years Ahead*, the gains reported by the N.A.I.C. were made in an unusually strong bull market prior to 1960, and, in any case, apply only to clubs which strictly followed the N.A.I.C. rules for investing.

New clubs come into existence every week, but others are constantly folding, and the membership of the surviving clubs is by no means stable.

There are a great many questions to be decided in any such club. What stocks shall be bought? When shall they be sold? When can the members expect an individual cash return on the $20 or $30 a month that each invests? Who shall make the decisions?

Usually decision-making is put in the hands of a

small committee, advised by someone connected with the stock market. For obvious reasons, that someone is likely to be a stockbroker. He may donate his time and counsel, but his interest in the club is not likely to be entirely gratuitous, or social. Some brokers handle the accounts of scores of clubs and, in such cases, commissions can run to very substantial sums.

Mutual Funds

Shortly after my first book was published, I received a call from the representative of one of Wall Street's largest investment-banking and brokerage houses. I was mystified, but agreed to discuss the proposition that the firm had in mind.

It developed that the company, thinking to cash in on the publicity attaching to my name as the result of my exploits in the stock market, wished to form a Darvas Fund—of which I would be the nominal head. From the investment bankers' point of view, I was a natural. The public, I was told, would flock in droves to buy shares in a mutual company headed by a man who had made $2,000,000 in Wall Street. After all, if I could select stocks for myself, why not for everyone?

It was an interesting and lucrative offer, but even if I had not had other commitments I would have said what I did say, which was—"No." Why? I told the company officers quite frankly that I could not even consider the offer, for the simple reason that I did not believe in mutual shares as an investment. In short, I was not going to ask people to put their money into something which I myself did not consider to be a good bet.

A mutual fund is an open-end investment trust company—open end because anyone can participate at any time (since new shares are always available), and he can redeem his shares at any time (because the fund stands ready to take them at the going market price).

The fund is organized along corporate lines, like any other business. Its stock in trade is money—the capital which the shareholders put into it, plus any profits. Its business is buying and selling the stocks of other businesses, hopefully at a profit on each transaction.

The price of the shares is fixed as the exact net asset value per share of the company (fund) at any given time, which seems reasonable enough. When you come to redeem your mutual shares, you will get what they are worth on a *pro rata* basis, in terms of the fund's own net worth of the moment. However, here comes the big "but."

It is the sales commission. This is a real, mansized bite, ranging on the average from 8.5 per cent to a whopping 9.5 or even 10 per cent. It is applied when I buy, and that means my invested dollar is worth 90 cents the minute I shake hands with my friendly mutual fund salesman. He's not there for his health.

Neither are the people who manage my money for me. All trust funds, including the open-enders, charge a management fee, ordinarily about one-half of one per cent per annum of the total amount of capital managed. That may not sound like such a big bite percentagewise. But when I consider a mutual fund group like Investors Diversified Services, Inc., controlling assets of more than $4 billion, I can understand what makes mutual funds interesting to the banking and brokerage industry.

There is still another factor to consider. Most big mutuals have close relationships with brokerage firms, and some are established by such firms. Here comes the dealer back into the game, cutting the pot on each transaction. A fund might do very well to make its investment and then let it ride, but stockbrokers need activity to make commissions, and when the mutual managers and the brokers are hand-in-glove, it will be questionable how much of the trading is legitimate and how much is merely churning for commissions.

Mutuals are big business. At last report there were 183 funds having assets in excess of $1,000,000 each. How well have they done for their stockholders? According to a survey by Kalb, Voorhis & Co., stockbrokers, only 18 of the 183 showed gains between March 29, 1962, and March 29, 1963. *Wellington Equity* fell off 14 per cent, as did *Putnam Growth*

Fund. The net assets of *Chase Fund* of Boston slid 26 per cent, *Peoples' Securities* fell 32 per cent, and *Imperial Fund* declined nearly 41 per cent.

Not all of the funds showed such dramatic losses, but I found that on the average, If I owned shares in any of the funds which had capital invested largely in common stocks (this does not include the 18 that showed gains mentioned above), my shares would *not* have done as well as the stock market averages, such as the Dow Jones industrial average.

Surprise! If I had invested in the *Dow Theory Fund*, I would have lost 18 per cent of my investment in a year.

The implications are plain. I would have done better during 1962-63 to follow the market averages than to put my money in the hands of professional managers, even if the professional management had been offered gratis. And of course it was not. Subtract 7.5 per cent to 8.5 per cent sales commission from the mutual balance sheet for the year, and then knock off another small fraction for the management fee, and it became clear why it is better for me to do my own gambling in the Wall Street casino.

Monthly Investment Plans

If someone were to invite me to play poker on the installment plan, I would ask to hear the punch line, because there is no such game. Yet the New York

Stock Exchange, with its Monthly Investment Plan, allowing investment in stocks for as little as $40 every three months, is really offering something almost as bizarre.

The big attraction is that it is painless saving—or it is supposed to be. The difference is that a savings bank will pay me up to 4 per cent or so for the use of my money. The brokers who handle my M.I.P. account will *charge* a full 6 per cent—and with no guarantee that my savings will still be there when I happen to need money. Dividends won't help much. If I buy stocks on the $40 a month plan, it will, in fact, be a full two years before my stock dividends have caught up with commissions—assuming that the average dividend is 3 to 4 per cent. And a lot of stocks don't pay anything like 3 per cent. I have no guarantee that I will get *any* dividend.

What's in Them for Main Street?

The investment clubs, the mutual funds, the monthly investment plans—all are part of the campaign to "bring Wall Street to Main Street," but whether Main Street benefits is another question. My own feeling is that the combines face the same hazards as the individual. If the methods used to select and buy and sell stocks are sound, a profit is possible, whether the stocks are bought on behalf of an individual or a group.

But gambling is gambling, and personally I would not care to let someone else make my bets for me, nor would I like to have to depend on the advice of the dealer in any game. From my point of view, we are on opposite sides of the table. I want profits from the market; he wants commissions—from me.

CHAPTER SIX

Playing in the Casino— My Buying Game

Some time ago I was in Paris in the spring, and as I sat at the café de la Paix watching the elegant women pass by—I am a confirmed stock-watcher but my history of girl-watching goes back even further—I read my broker's message with an air of gloom. I had reached a crisis in my financial career and was on a depressing losing streak.

Because I am serious about the stock market, I kept thinking to myself, "Yes, yes, buying and selling is a gamble." Certainly my chequered career showed me that! But how could I minimize those gambles and risks? Surely I could think of *some* way to select the right stocks and buy and sell them at the right time. That was my problem in a nutshell. I wanted to de-

129

velop a system that would be foolproof. I was Jason looking for the Golden Fleece.

I reviewed in my mind some of my observations of the market.

In the Wall Street casino I had observed a variety of games; where the prizes and the odds varied. Conditions and even the rules of the various games change —or are changed by the management. (Remember how the American Stock Exchange ruled out stop-loss orders after *How I Made $2,000,000 in the Stock Market* was published?) And the players—here I speak of the relatively small handful of successful speculators, as against the uninformed and wishful majority—take different approaches to the same problems, each according to the objectives which he has set for himself, his psychology, the conditions under which he finds that *he,* personally, can operate most successfully.

The short seller, for instance, plays a role analogous to that of the "wrong" bettor at the dice table—the gambler who never rolls the dice himself, but uses his understanding of the percentages to find his advantage in covering the bets of the other players.

Playing the market is vastly more complex than dice or Twenty-One, but the same principles apply.

The rules which I worked out for myself in Wall Street were discovered and refined in a certain sort of market, for a certain sort of player—namely, myself. No doubt there are other equally valid methods.

Although there is no such thing as "can't" in the

stock market, and any stock can go in any direction at any time, nevertheless, the price movements of stocks are, by their very nature, limited. I decided to concentrate my attentions on this movement in all its variations.

The accomplished horse race handicapper does not waste his time playing roulette, except as a social pastime. The rare card expert with a phenomenal memory and thorough understanding of the odds of blackjack doesn't throw his money away at the dice table. I wanted to play in this casino and win. So I set myself the task of knowing the game thoroughly.

I found out that the first secret of success in Wall Street—as well as elsewhere—was having self-discipline and patience. I had to wait until the opportunity came to play my game, not someone else's. The compulsive gambler may play for pennies with the children on the street corner when nothing better offers. But as the operator who is bucking the casino—not for excitement, but with rational goals and a method—I had to approach it coldly, with my eyes open. I knew that I would have to learn to wait a year if necessary for a single winning coup; and that I could not afford, under any circumstance, to dribble my capital away on compromises that negated the principles of my system.

I developed what became known as the Darvas Method in a rising market—what Wall Street refers to as a "bull" market. That means, in the simplest terms, a market in which there is strong buyer interest.

In this bull market, although some stocks were rising and others declining in price, many more were going UP than were going DOWN. In a so-called "bear" market, by contrast, the opposite would have been true: there would have been decreasing demand, more willingness to sell at progressively lower prices (another way of saying less *support* for stocks), and more stocks going DOWN than going UP.

Although I have been able to make money in almost any kind of a market—and often I find myself in a "mixed" one, I have learned that my best trading comes when I can take advantage of the dramatic opportunities of the bull market. Because I was out to beat the casino, I wanted to develop a "system" or method that would work for me.

I Developed My Box System

During my initiation into the stock market, I was absolutely in the dark about even the barest mechanics of stock buying and selling. I had no idea who bought stocks, or why. I saw no reason why some stocks should go UP in price, and others go DOWN. Everything I did was guesswork, gambling of the wildest sort, based on tips, rumors, advice from people who knew no more than I did but managed to sound as if they might. Except for that lucky break with the BRILUND mining stock in Toronto that got me into the market, I lost

132

almost every round. I was the greenest greenhorn in the casino.

In time I realized that if I was going to survive I would have to *know* what kind of game it was that I was playing, and at least the elementary rules. But the "fundamentals" that I learned proved almost as useless as the tips on which I had previously relied. I was misled by the commonly held myths about the stock market to which even brokers and reputable "market analysts" subscribe. Instead of paying attention to what the stocks themselves were doing, I studied the financial affairs of the companies that issued the stocks, and it took me some while to realize that I was looking in the wrong place for the information I really needed.

What I wanted to know was simple enough: Which stocks were going to go UP and make money for me?

Corporation reports could tell me how much the companies in question were earning annually, how much steel JONES & LAUGHLIN was producing, how many oil wells PACIFIC PETROLEUM owned, and so on. Stockbrokers could resurrect the Wall Street *past* for me, all the way back to Moxie and highbutton shoes.

But what nobody seemed able to tell me anything about was the *future,* and it was not until I stumbled onto TEXAS GULF PRODUCING that I found my first real clue.

My investment in 1,000 shares of TEXAS GULF PRODUCING was made in absolute desperation. I had just dropped $9,000 on JONES & LAUGHLIN, was in debt up to my eyebrows, and had to recoup or go broke. At that sorry stage of affairs, who could have foreseen that I would make over $2,000,000 in the stock market? But I was lucky. TEXAS GULF PRODUCING produced handsomely, and put me back on my financial feet again. Far more important, it taught me a basic lesson. I had bought the stock for one reason, and one reason only. It seemed to be rising. Subsequent experience confirmed the lesson.

I was to repeat it many times over with predictable success, and on this basis I decided that MY ONLY SOUND REASON FOR BUYING A STOCK IS THAT IT IS RISING IN PRICE. IF THAT IS HAPPENING, NO OTHER REASON IS REQUIRED. IF THAT IS NOT HAPPENING, NO OTHER REASON IS WORTH CONSIDERING.

Having grasped the principle just stated, I had won half the battle. But I still had a long way to go. How could I distinguish a stock which is *surely* rising from the many others which may register gains of a point or two one week, only to surrender it the next? How would I know the difference between those occasional stocks which are tugging at their tethers and about to soar upwards like liberated balloons, and the many which bob up and down in the ocean of indecision, or scuttle sideways across the chart like crippled crabs? In short, how could I *spot* trends?

In the process of answering these questions, I made an intensive study of the day-to-day and week-to-week price movements of hundreds of individual stocks.

My tools were these:

Graphic Stocks, published by F. W. Stephens, New York, in two volumes; one containing more than a thousand charts, showing the price movements of stocks, with monthly high and low prices for more than 11 years; the other volume charting a group of 81 of the best-known stocks over a period of 30 years.

A Standard & Poor's stock guide (which I obtained from my broker at no cost,) listing high and low prices, earnings, dividends, and other statistical data for some 4,800 common and preferred stocks, from 1936 to date.

Barron's weekly financial publication, for price movements of stocks on the Big Board and Amex.

The *Wall Street Journal* for day-to-day changes.

Long and painstaking study of actual price movements, as against the usually irrelevant and confusing welter of statistics offered in annual reports and stockbrokers' tip sheets, showed me something that I had not previously realized.

It was that, contrary to my impression, stocks behaved with a certain consistency, following upward or downward trends, which made it possible to foresee what they were *likely to do* on the basis of what they *actually were doing.*

Although there was considerable diversity in the day-to-day and even hour-to-hour movements of any active stock—and clearly I was not interested in any other kind—all tended to follow certain characteristic patterns of behavior over the longer run. I became fascinated—even obsessed—with the casino and its workings.

I saw stocks go up and stocks go down. Movement—*movement* was the keyword. Once a trend was established, either up or down, it continued to move in that direction, as though drawn by powerful magnets. I saw reasons for this; buying tended to generate more buying and progressively higher prices. Conversely, selling at a given price soon exhausts the supply of buyers available at that price, and forces offerings at a lower price—and this process, too, tends to be progressive.

Be that as it may, I saw that few stocks shoot up like rockets without pausing on the way, and few plummet like stones on their downward course. In both directions, there is stiffening resistance at various levels.

Examining the stock charts, I could see the effects of this resistance in graphic form. A stock would rise to a certain level. Then, as though running into a ceiling, it would rebound like a tennis ball, hit a floor in the downward direction, and again bounce upwards, only to run, again, into the same resistance as before.

I began to see that the effect was to set up an oscillating movement within narrowly defined limits, like a rubber ball bouncing inside of a glass box. And that is precisely what I began to see in my mind's eye—no longer stocks flying in all directions like bats in a belfry, but orderly progression, the rhythm varying with each individual stock, yet the movement in each case sufficiently regular and predictable to be mentally charted and understood.

Viewed haphazardly from day to day, the price movements of stocks made no sense. One day a stock might open at 35, reach a high for the day of 38, and close at 37, for a net gain of 2 points. The next day it might continue to rise, or it might equally well beat a retreat to 34, 33. . . . Who could tell *where* it would stop?

But studying the longer-range trends, I could see, barely at first, but then stronger—Eureka!—there was method in this madness—or at least some semblance of order. The stock which had varied by three points in a day I discovered to have, over a period of two weeks or so, a spread of a full eight points—from a low of 30 to a high of 38. Looking back still farther into the records I confirmed what I had begun to suspect. Until a certain date, the stock had moved in a lower price range, three or four times reaching 30, but never topping it. Then one day it had made a breakthrough, and had not stopped moving upward until it had touched a new ceiling, 38. Since then it had bounced between these two figures, 30 as the low, and 38 as the high, and these figures provided the limits of its bouncing movement. It had, in other words, moved into a new box—a 30/38 box.

Was I on the verge of a discovery? I felt a little like Galileo, but I kept watch.

Still further checking revealed that the entire upward progress of the stock in question had consisted of movements of a similar sort—a progression from one box to another, each stage in the development of the stock being marked by a period of oscillation between clearly discernible limits, then a breakthrough, and a new period of bouncing up and down in the next box, and so on.

The long-range price movement, then, was not erratic, as it seemed on casual inspection, but consisted of a *series of movements* which I could visualize as a tall stack of boxes, one atop the other. The oscillation which occurred for a longer or shorter term within each box marked a stage in the progress of the stock, a gathering of forces, so to speak, before a new assault on the next line of resistance and the onward march to the next stage, upward or downward, in continuance of the established trend.

I had stumbled on a revelation. It was like finding the key to a cryptogram; the master panel that controls the lighting effects on a stage.

The application of the box theory was a relatively simple matter, although it took some experimentation, and I made miscalculations along the way.

My first step was to work out a method to establish, beyond doubt, the limits of my boxes, so as not to mistake the price fluctuations *within* a box for the transition to the next higher—or lower—box.

In mentally charting swiftly developing stocks, this is not always easy. Eventually, I learned from experience to rely on a rule which has proved itself to be almost invariably accurate.

When reviewing stocks with an eye to spotting trends, I checked the price changes on a weekly basis, in *Barron's.* A rapid glance through three or four back issues, up to the latest, was enough for me to determine the price range within which a given stock was fluctuating.

However, when a stock was in transition, I kept an accurate *daily* check on its fluctuations, taking note of two all-important factors. One was the *highest* price paid for the stock during the day's trading. The other was the low for the day.

While a stock was still running, its movement looked something like this:

Open	High	Low	Close	Net Change
35	37	34¼	37	+2
37	38	36	37½	+ ½
37	41	36	40	+3

In such a pattern there was a consistent rise. Each day's high was higher than that of the day before, and I would leave the top of the box still open. The sky could be the limit.

Usually, though, I found that it was a limited rise.

139

After a while, the buy orders which had created the boom decreased, the energy which had gone into the rise dissipated, and the stock would run out of steam temporarily.

Then I found that the high of each succeeding day failed to reach, or in any case failed to exceed, that of the previous day.

The pattern looked something like this:

High	Low	Close	Net Change
41	37	40	−1
40½	37	40½	+ ½
40½	36½	40¼	− ¼

When I saw that the stock had failed to reach its previous peak (in the example above it would be 41) for three consecutive days, the TOP of the box could be established. It was that same peak, representing the level of resistance at which no buyers were found became the new ceiling which was to be broken before the stock could be expected to take off again.

Having established a new ceiling, the stock was now to be expected to react as sales, usually representing a certain amount of profit taking, went into effect. To establish the BOTTOM of the box, all I did was to observe the lowest point at which the stock sold in the following days. The new bottom was established by observing the *lowest* price to which the stocks dipped but did not penetrate over *three consecutive days.*

In the example just given, the top of the new box was 36½, and so I placed the stock in a narrow 36½/41 box, with the daily prices bouncing back and forth between these two figures until I noticed sufficient energy was generated for a new breakthrough, signaling a new rise. I felt like a child with a new toy.

I Used My Box System

All right now, I said to myself. I've got my boxes and I've established the limits. But what will I do now? Does the box tell me when to buy and sell? I puzzled this out. In theory my box method was a good tool. It told me about the development of individual stocks and thus was useful except in periods of rapid change when things were going too fast to define the limits of growth or decline.

By my practice, I found that my methods were best suited to the sort of market in which the greatest opportunity for selection over a wide range of rapidly rising stocks existed—and that, of course, meant a strong bull market.

As I progressed, I became increasingly more selective. I realized that I could seldom expect to know—in time to act—just *why* a stock should be pushing its way upward from one box to the next, while another issue in the same industry group seemed to be doing just the opposite. But since I was more interested in effects than in causes, *I did not greatly care!* What was

141

important to me was to be able to see the trend, and to take full advantage of it. Furthermore, I was interested in *maximum* growth.

This being the case, it seemed only logical to choose those stocks that had already showed what they could do by actually doing it. In short, I determined that I would look at stocks as though they were horses in a race, and judge them on form. That meant automatically throwing out the also-rans, even though they might have been front-runners at some earlier period, and concentrating on those few that were actually surpassing themselves, with no sign of flagging.

This is how I figured: A stock which which was formerly a champion, selling at, say 150, may look like a bargain if it is currently on the market at 40 and gaining ground. But I also figured that it is coming from behind, and thus laboring at a terrific handicap. To have slipped back from 150 to 40 means to have inevitably inflicted serious losses on all the traders who bought it at or near the peak and were later forced to sell at lower prices. Thus there is certain to be strong psychological resistance to overcome, much ground to regain, before such a stock will again begin to look like a winner.

Viewed this way I felt that the stock that has lost ground is in exactly the same position as the champion who has fallen behind in a race. Before he can begin to win, he must first make up the ground he has lost. Some entries may be able to come from behind.

142

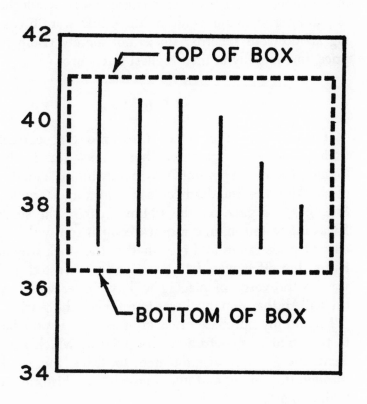

But in my opinion, few race horses, or runners, and very few stocks, have enough "push" in them to do it.

Following somewhat this line of reasoning, I came to the conclusion that the only stocks which would be of real interest to me would be those that were breaking all previous records: stocks not merely rising in price, but actually in their highest boxes ever.

When I Bought

It wasn't too long before I realized that correct timing is vital. To know whether a stock was in the topmost box of the pyramid was merely for me a matter of checking the Standard & Poor's index and *Graphic Stocks*. These gave me the all-time peak of the stock I was interested in, and a quick comparison with the current price range told me whether the stock was in its top box. If it was, I became really interested and was on the verge of placing a "buy" order with my broker. All that remained was to establish the price.

I found my purchase price, at or as near as possible to the point of penetration—the point at which sufficient energy was accumulated to drive the stock *through* the ceiling and into a new box on historically high ground.

Thus, in a stock in the 36¾/41 box (assuming that 40 was the all-time previous high mark for the issue), I placed a purchase order when I saw clear indication of a penetration of the 41 ceiling, when the daily *high*

had actually pushed even a fraction through the 41
ceiling for *three consecutive days*—no matter what
the closing price was each day.

How I Bought

The use of the word "automatically" is apropos to
this discussion, because it describes, precisely, the
kind of transaction which I found to be imperative, if
I was not to lose important profits.

While I was still working out the box system, I
found occasion to apply it to a stock called LOUISIANA
LAND & EXPLORATION. The price had been rising steadily for some weeks, working its way upward from one
box to the next. When it seemed to have established
itself in its topmost box, with a ceiling of 59¾, I
decided to buy. I telephoned my broker, and told him
to let me know the moment the stock reached 61,
which I considered to be the correct "buy" level.

The call came, but I could not be reached for two
hours. By the time my broker finally got through to
me on the telephone, LOUISIANA LAND & EXPLORATION
was being quoted at 63. I had already lost two points,
which, for my intended purchase of 100 shares, would
have meant $200 in my pocket, within a matter of
hours.

The stock confirmed my judgment by continuing to
climb. In my excitement and annoyance at having
missed getting in at the bottom, I compounded my

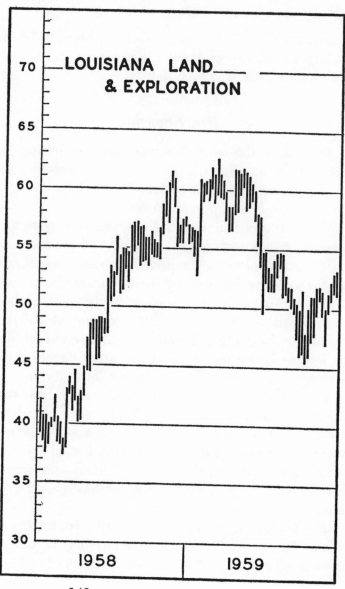

LOUISIANA LAND
& EXPLORATION

mistake by buying at 65—which proved to be the TOP of the new box.

It was an expensive error, but possibly worthwhile, because, when I came to discuss it with my broker, he was able to provide the remedy. In the future, when I knew what stock I wished to buy and at what price, I was to ask him to put in an on-stop purchase order, which would *automatically* go into force when my stock reached the DESIRED LEVEL.

Subsequent experience proved the wisdom of this decision. In my next three transactions, I made a profit of $2,442,36. The transactions were:

ALLEGHENY LUDLUM STEEL—200 shares, bought as it moved into the $\boxed{45/50}$ box at 45¾, and sold three weeks later at 51.

COPPER-BESSEMER—300 shares, bought on the edge of the $\boxed{40/50}$ box at 40¾, and sold at 45⅛.

DRESSER INDUSTRIES—300 shares, bought at 84 when it seemed to be moving into the $\boxed{84/92}$ box, and sold at 85½ when it failed to move up through the new box as quickly as I thought it should.

The on-stop buy-order was a big step forward, a proven automatic weapon in my growing arsenal. My artillery had previously included my technique of selecting a stock which had surpassed or was on the point of surpassing its all-time high price, and establishing the upper limits of its box by observing the point at which the quotation approached (but did not penetrate for *three consecutive days*) the all-

147

time high. Now I had the big gun—placing my on-stop purchase order at the closest fraction above the level where the breakthrough would come.

I Learned to Select the Right Stock

For me, as with many others, time itself is money, and so naturally I want to put my capital where it will produce the biggest pay-off in the least time; if not, I would be investing in old-law tenements, or Christmas tree acreage, or any one of a number of money makers immensely more secure than common stocks.

I tried to get a system of selecting stocks. New highs are recorded every day in Wall Street and I could not buy all of them and I would not wish to. It became necessary for me to be selective, to whittle down that list, keeping in mind that one real producer, a phenomenal issue like, say THIOKOL, on which I made close to three-quarters of a million dollars, is worth scores of lesser stocks. I was not interested in the sprinter, that would make a speedy hundred-yard dash and then quit. It was a champion that would run and keep on running, that interested me.

Early in the game I worked out a method of making a rough selection of stocks—to be considered on their merits, not necessarily bought—that has saved me a great deal of time poring over the record books.

Once a week I took the latest copy of *Barron's* to a

148

quiet secluded spot and perused the statistical section, where the stock prices for the past week were listed.

To the left of each column of stock names and prices for the week there are two narrow columns of figures, representing the high and low prices paid for each stock during the current year. (For the first quarter, the list will cover the activity of the previous year.)

With pen in hand, I zoomed rapidly down the page, mentally comparing the highs and lows. When I saw a high for the year that was at least *double* the corresponding low figure (in other words, a 100 per cent advance), I automatically glanced across the page to the stock's high for the week. If it was at or within a few points of the high for the year, I made a check mark at the outside of the column, and continued to read through the listings in the same manner.

Within a quarter of an hour I had culled my rough selections for the week. The remaining stocks were chaff, and could safely be ignored.

My rough selections were not, of course, to be bought without further checking.

I next looked up the rough selections in Standard & Poor's index, or in *Graphic Stocks,* or both. In the majority of cases, the stocks on my list, although at or near their peak prices for the year, were not at their *historical* peaks. Those that failed this important test were automatically tossed out—however attractive they seemed.

I then subjected them to further tests, but these

149

were largely dependent on judgment and no absolute
rules could be laid down for them.

I Checked Volume as a Clue

In general, I noted that stocks which were about
to be launched to new price levels showed a stepped-
up volume of activity, indicating increased interest on
the part of traders. Small volume indicated little interest. On the other hand, large volume was not
significant, in connection with popular stocks like
GENERAL MOTORS or INTERNATIONAL TELEPHONE & TELE-
GRAPH, of which millions of shares are outstanding and
hundreds of thousands of shares change hands weekly.

I looked for remarkably increased volume in a stock
in which trading had been relatively quiet. My philosophy was that unusual behavior of any sort was always
meaningful, whether in stocks or in human beings. In
a quiet person, a wild burst of energy is an indication
that something has happened to him—if a staid alder-
man breaks into song at the dinner table, you can take
it that he has either received very good news, or has
been drinking. I figured that in a placid, little-traded
stock, a sudden spurt of activity could be taken as a
sign that people behind the scenes had decided—for
whatever mysterious reasons of their own—that the
stock which heretofore was of little interest was about
to become a good buy. I didn't know *why* they thought
so—and by the time I could find out it would probably
be too late to act. But the fact that they thought so was

sufficient to me, because insiders—like outsiders—act on their belief. And it is their buying, not their thinking that will, in my belief, boost the price of the stock.

Stock Fundamentals

I have many friends in the Market and when we get together socially we always discuss business—to the distress of the ladies. We may all look the same in our suits but underneath we tend to fall into two opposing camps.

On the one side are the men who judge the future of a stock by the financial data relating to the issuing corporation. Such men are called *fundamentalists,* because they guide themselves by so-called fundamentals. On the other side I found those who judge what a stock is likely to do by observing the actual performance of that stock. Their clues to the market are technical clues, and so they are known as *technicians.* The longer I became involved with the affairs of that unpredictable, multi-billion-dollar mile known as Wall Street, the less confidence I had in the so-called fundamentals of stocks, and the more faith I developed in simple observation—my own, let me add—of the stocks themselves.

I did not, however, consider *all* basic information relating to companies and industries as worthless in the stock market.

Obviously, if I learned that a diamond as big as the Ritz had been discovered, unbeknownst to Wall Street, immediately beneath Madison Square Garden, I would call my broker and tell him to buy all the MADISON SQUARE GARDEN stock he could lay hands on at the going price.

I also considered other factors such as capitalization. I consulted Standard & Poor's, where I found out how many shares of common stock (and preferred stock, if any) the company had issued. Obviously this was vital information for me to judge accurately the volume of trading activity in a given stock. What was small volume for GENERAL MOTORS, with 283,000,000 common shares outstanding, was, for example, tremendous volume for PACIFIC PETROLEUM, with little more than 16,000,000 shares issued, and half of that held by PHILLIPS PETROLEUM.

Despite what most market analysts believe, or told me they believe, I found it hard to see why company earnings should have any important effect on the price of a stock. I know that earnings have some bearing on the dividends to be paid, but I could earn as much or more, with far greater security, in any savings bank.

Nevertheless I found out by simple observation that trust funds, investment trusts, and other big institutional buyers have to put their money—and the profit on their investments—into *some* stock. And nine times out of ten their decision is based primarily on the magical earnings-to-price ratio in which Wall Street so devoutly believes.

I felt that the logical result of investment capital

following the trail of earnings produces price increases in those stocks with the best earnings record or, better said, with the greatest *expectation* of increasing earnings. I found that in choosing among stocks—all other factors being equal—the one with the greatest attraction in terms of actual or prospective earnings would be my best bet, because a lot of traders will be buying it, and their collective decision will be certain to boost the price.

For sound psychological reasons, I decided that I wanted to know no more than I absolutely needed to know about the affairs of corporations in whose stocks I was interested. It is all too easy to be influenced by factors that don't matter.

Nevertheless, I had to know whether a chosen stock was tied to the affairs of a static or dying industry. As I saw it, it might be that somewhere there is a good buy in the stock of a buggy whip manufacturing company. But since there are no longer enough buggies being used to create any great demand for buggy whips, the buggy whip stock is not going to create much of a ripple on Wall Street, unless the news gets about that the buggy whip firm has received some big government contracts for radio-telescope antennae, or something with an equally promising future.

In selecting my stocks, then, I found I took a longer-range view than a purely technical approach to the stock market would suggest.

It was when I was in London that I actually got it

down on paper. I had literally doodled myself a workable market theory and it had been snatched away from me under protest. I was at the theatre seeing a dull British musical and during the intermission the usherette handed me my tea-tray. Marvelously civilized custom! Not wanting to drink the tepid tea I took out a pencil and scratch pad and scribbled the following:

Method of stock investment

Technical	*Fundamental*
Box system	Capitalization
Volume	Industry Group
Historical Peak Price Related to Present Price	Expected Earnings
On-Stop Buy-Order	

The more I looked at my jottings the more it became apparent to me that my method was a fusion of the two. As the musicians returned to the pit, I was trying to coin an official name for my method. Technimental? Not so good. Fundical? Ridiculous. Technofund? Dullish. Techno-fundamentalist. That sounded pretty good. A neighbor of mine asked to see my program and as I handed it over, turning away, the efficient usherette whisked away my tray, cold tea, biscuit, and newly discovered financial system. So one thing I know for sure. I may not be the only techno-fundamentalist around.

CHAPTER SEVEN

Playing in the Casino— My Selling Game

a PHILOSOPHER would say that it is unreasonable to expect great rewards without being willing to take great risks. Yet the constant goal of the intelligent entrepreneur in any field is to reduce the risks while greatly increasing the rewards.

It is human nature to wish it, and we know that it can be done, or there would be no self-made millionaires. A perusal of *Who's Who* reveals that there are many, many people who have made their fortunes in the stock market.

For me, the risk-reduction factor was foremost in my mind at all times. I wanted to make a lot of money, yes—for the independence it would give me, and because of the wonderful challenge that beating the Wall Street casino presented. But I was even more anxious not to lose the money that was already mine.

I was endowed—whether for good or ill—with a native realism which told me that if I bought a stock at $100 and the price declined to $90, I would no longer be the possessor of $100, but of a stock certificate with a market value of $90 (less commissions). To look at the matter any other way would be the worst sort of wishful thinking. I could not pretend to myself that $100 of mine had gone on a little vacation and would soon return. The unwelcome reality would be that *my* money—all $100 of it—would be in the pockets of the seller and the brokers. It would no longer be mine. What I would have in exchange would be a certificate formerly quoted at $100 and now worth $90. Or $80. Or $70. Who knows what the price will be next week? Next month? Next year?

Reasoning along these lines, I could see very clearly that I could afford to own only one kind of stocks— those actually rising in price or giving promise of doing so in the immediate future, that promise being based on strong performance to date. To hold a declining stock was to indulge in day-dreaming while watching useful capital melt before my eyes.

My market philosophy was not to buy cheap and sell dear, as the Wall Street maxim has it, but to buy stocks going UP, and to sell stocks going DOWN—the sooner the better.

There are traders who live with a telephone in their hand, and at one point in my career this was my situation. I was calling my broker literally every fifteen minutes to ask, "How's Lorillard? How's Polaroid?" People with nothing else to do, and a passion for gambling, sit all day in the board rooms of big brokerage houses, watching the ticker, reading news bulletins which may or may not have some effect on the hour-to-hour market, and exchanging rumors.

I found that, for myself, proximity to Wall Street was fatal. I was too easily swayed by the minor fluctuations of the market, the talk about impending mergers, acquisitions, splits; I could never stick to any sort of system while under such influences.

Rather, it was during my absences from New York, and especially during the two years of a tour that took me around the world, when I found myself operating most profitably.

In New York, practically at my broker's elbow, it seemed that everything I did was wrong. I was nervous, impatient, fearful. I bought some stocks too late, sold others too soon.

Away on the other side of the world, in Tokyo, Saigon, or Kathmandu in Nepal, where my only link with Wall Street was the uncertain telegraph service reluctantly provided by the Indian Legation, I regained my perspective.

Back copies of *Barron's*, arriving a week or more late, showed me what stocks had been *doing*, rather than what was being said about them. Rumors fell away. The daily columns of analysis, giving plausible but unreliable explanations for each little dip or rise in price, were seen for what they were—so much guesswork. The brief daily quotations which I received by cable from my broker, containing only the essentials concerning stocks in which I had an immediate interest—the high, low, and closing prices for each day —told me all I needed to know. Used in conjunction with *Barron's,* the daily quotations enabled me to apply my box system far better than I could have if I had been sitting in a board room in lower Manhattan. The reason, of course, was that—removed from the scene—I could see the characteristic patterns of stock behavior, stripped of all that was extraneous and irrelevant to my purpose.

However, to see clearly is only half of the battle. In order to avoid being locked into a market that might decline just as suddenly as it might rise, I had to be ready to sell any stock the moment it showed signs of slipping into a lower box. In New York, it was simply a matter of telephoning my broker. In Kathmandu, I had to have an *automatic* safety device—something that would sell me out of a given stock at the first sign of danger, whether or not I happened to be able to reach my broker.

That indispensable safety device was the STOP-LOSS ORDER, the second and most important of the automatic weapons in my armory.

Without it, I was dependent on communications that were unreliable and often nonexistent for hours or days at a time. With it, the box system was perfect. I could work thousands of miles from Wall Street, not merely as well as if I had been on the scene, but actually *better* than if I had been there. And best of all, I could go to bed each night knowing that, no matter what happened in Wall Street, I was not sleeping while my losses mounted. Any stock that slipped from its box was *automatically* sold, close to the price at which I myself would have sold it had I been my own broker, operating on the very floor of the exchange.

There is nothing complicated about the stop-loss order. Like the on-stop buy-order, it is simply an order given in advance, transmitted by the commission broker to the specialist who handles the particular stock, instructing him to sell out when the stock falls to a predetermined price.

How I Applied the Stop-Loss Order

I continued to buy stocks at the nearest fraction above the point of upward penetration. My theory, backed by observation of the characteristic behavior of hundreds of individual stocks, told me that so long as the stock remained within the confines of its box —in other words, so long as the price remained within the range which the action of the market had estab-

159

lished for it—I would not be concerned by the hourly or daily fluctuations peculiar to it. But the moment the stock penetrated the price ceiling from which it had hitherto rebounded, I bought. I bought because it had been my experience that, once a stock moved out of its box in an upward direction, it could *continue* to rise until the accumulated buying power which had pushed it through its previous price ceiling has been expended.

When a stock broke out of the top of its box, I thought I should jump into action because something in the situation had *changed*. The new upward movement was motivated by the pressure of rapidly expanded buyer demand—never mind the reasons for the rising demand—thrusting the price up, just as steam gathering behind a piston head builds up pressure until it has reached a point of compression at which it suddenly thrusts the piston forward.

But, on the other side of the coin, I also found that when a stock which had been bouncing securely inside its box suddenly slipped, I had to infer that the fact that it had had a bottom showed that something was supporting the price. But whatever the nature of the support—which I did not really need to know about—when this support was withdrawn I knew that something significant must have happened. And I sold because I had no way of telling, once the bottom fell out of the box, how far the price might fall or when

160

rallying support at a lower level would stop the plunge.

Contrary to what others told me, I saw nothing to gain and much to lose by holding a declining stock, when each point lost meant a thousand dollars or more, and the hope of recovery was like a gambler's wishful thinking. I wanted to sell, *to stop my loss,* at the precise moment at which I was certain that the downward movement had begun. *That point was the point of penetration at the bottom of the box.*

A stock might bounce against the bottom of its box as often as it pleased. In fact, I considered that the bounce had a healthy effect, like a sprinter about to take off jumps up and down to limber up. It provided the energy for an even stronger rebound, by shaking out the timid or uncertain traders whose profit-taking would otherwise weaken the upward progress of the stock, once it really began to rise.

Thus, if a stock was in the 35/40 box, I did not care how often it hit 35. But the moment that it fell through the bottom of the box, I got rid of it, because I knew that something had happened to weaken its support, and I could not predict how far it would fall before it would reach a new, lower level of support, and establish itself in a new box.

I would then place the stop-loss order at the nearest fraction below the bottom of the box, after determining carefully, of course, the dimensions of that box.

Actually, I made use of my stop-loss order like a

161

gambler who holds off his good card until it becomes really necessary to lay it on the table. I used my stop-loss order as a net. Very often I bought stocks in full confidence that they would rise—a new stock like a new broom sweeps clean, I thought, but not always. So when this newly purchased stock thumbed its nose at me and turned downward, I wanted to limit my losses. Thus the stop-loss served as a kind of safety net, an automatic circuit breaker that cut my loss a fraction point below my purchase price. It helped me sleep better too. I could buy new stock, leave the country, forget about it and know that I would be always covered.

A young lawyer, who was a good friend of mine and shared my interest in the market, lunched with me one day at Longchamps and we got into our usual argument about my methods which he—Harvard trained—considered very unorthodox. "You're just always lucky," he said. I tried to explain. "Look," I said and, drawing out a pencil, started to illustrate on the Longschamps tablecloth what I meant. "Let me take a stock in the $\boxed{35/40}$ box by way of illustration, and say, for the sake of simplicity, that 40 also represents the historical peak price. From observing the characteristic movement of stocks and the box system, I know that, once the stock has broken through 40, it will be on a definite uptrend and should be bought at this point. Therefore I place an on-stop buy order at 40⅛. Since observation also assures me that a stock

162

which has moved up into a new high box is unlikely to fall below its point of penetration (unless the trend is definitely reversed) I will place, simultaneously with my on-stop buy-order at $40\frac{1}{8}$ a stop-loss order at $39\frac{7}{8}$. For my purposes, until the dimensions of a new, higher box can be determined, $39\frac{7}{8}$ becomes the safety line —the point at which I will consider that the stock is backsliding, and will sell."

For me, the stop-loss has always been a safety net, and like a steeplejack, working at dangerous heights, I always had it behind me as I climbed. If I fell, the net was there; I never fell more than a single story—or in this case, a single box.

I realized always that the stop-loss was valuable as a safety net, but it had other values as well. I had learned through experience at what point to buy and that was well and good. But the knack of when to sell was harder to get at.

In charting the course of stocks by the box system, I saw the rising trend. What I could not see, and could not guess, was when the stock would reach its peak.

My compromise was to sell as near as possible to the peak—specifically, that point at which the stock had reached its top box, reversed itself and gave sure indication of entering a downward trend by slipping through the bottom of the top box. To make sure that I sold within a few points of that peak, all I did was *raise* the stop-loss order simultaneously with the stock's rise. I didn't hit the absolute peak price on the nose, although I always came within fractions of it.

This automatic close-out method was my way of setting up the odds in my favor, of reducing my losses to a minimum, of cashing in my chips before it was too late, and protecting my winnings. And the house paid off!

How the Automatic Close-Out Made Me a Minor Prophet

Many times I have been pointed out as "The Man Who Made $2,000,000 in the Stock Market." I could equally well be called "The Man Who Predicted the Crash"; or a Minor Prophet, because my system foresaw the Big Slump of May 30, 1962, and I was, for practical purposes, out of the market *four and a half months in advance*. But that might serve to overemphasize the importance of the slump. In fact, the May, 1962, market was long overdue for what the experts call a "correction," and a brief study of any long-term stock chart told me that the market was, by its very nature, a boom-and-bust proposition, with a fairly regular rhythm of "bullish" and "bearish" sessions. There was nothing really unusual about the '62 crash except its dimensions. Stock prices plunged farther than usual because they had risen to far greater heights than in the past. They had farther to fall.

Brokers and market "analysts" like to talk about the stock market in general terms, as though it were some sort of intelligent or at least emotional entity, with its moods, its depressions, its bursts of euphoria, its varying states of health or anemia. It is a picturesque way to talk, but such references are merely figures of speech.

In truth, there is no such animal as "the stock market," either as bull or as bear. There is simply a big casino (and various smaller ones) in which thousands of avid gamblers and a few cool heads wager, with their own chips. When there are more optimists than pessimists betting on a given issue, that issue rises in price. If the reverse situation, the issue goes down. If more issues slump than rise, we talk about a "bear" market. It is all like a very complicated version of the match game.

For me the only way to win was to observe *how* the betting was going. I place a wager that it will keep on going that way and stipulate (by stop-loss order) that the wager is off if it doesn't.

Those who have reason to make it look more complicated than it is like to talk in generalities. There is much written, for example, about the "over-all growth" of the stock market—meaning stocks in general—as measured by such standards as the Dow Jones industrial average of 30 selected issues.

To some extent, I was influenced by this sort of thinking, and perhaps rightly so, because there *is* a psychological connection between the averages and the performance of individual stocks. When traders

165

believe that "the market" is going sour, they become hesitant to buy *any* stock.

But it does not necessarily follow that, when the situation was reversed and the averages were rising, all I had to do was get on the bandwagon. In a "rising market" it is certain that many stocks will be going up. Otherwise the averages obviously could not rise. But even when the averages were booming I saw that many stocks were going DOWN. Individual stocks constantly move back and forth, from one category to the other, every week, every day, often from one minute to the next.

One of my brokers told me, by way of sales talk, that investment in common stocks was the best way to beat inflation; since the Dow Jones and other averages have risen over the years to keep pace with or to move ahead of inflated prices elsewhere—while fixed income from savings, interest on bonds, and so on, have not kept pace and the invested capital remains the same.

This is superficial analysis, because it is based on an abstraction—something that does not exist except as a concept. The Dow Jones industrial average is much higher today than it was twenty years ago, true. But what is overlooked is that the 30 stocks from which the index is computed are not necessarily the same stocks from year to year. Those that decline are left by the wayside. New issues are substituted.

The averages are rising. That's nice. But what about

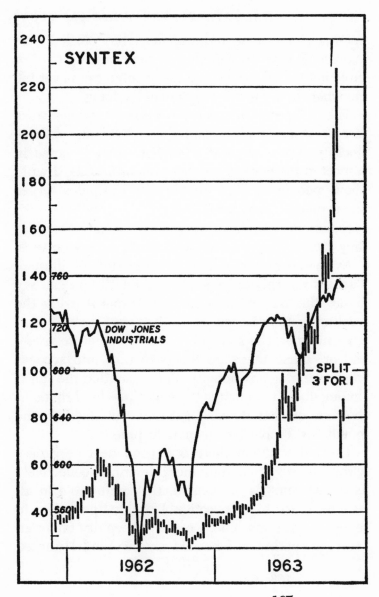

SYNTEX

DOW JONES
INDUSTRIALS

SPLIT
3 FOR 1

1962   1963

my stock? I cannot, unfortunately, buy stock in the average. I have to gamble on some one, or two, or three individual issues. And the average can never tell me what these specific issues may be doing.

The difference between the averages, which are a sort of Platonic ideal, and the individual, concrete stocks recalls a classical reference. Aristotle noted in respect to the work of another famous Greek: "I write about people as they *should be;* Euripides writes about them as they *are.*"

Experience taught me to pay attention to stocks as they are, judging each on its individual performance.

As to the averages, they are the stuff of illusion. There is no truly average stock. And all you can say about "the market," as a concept, is that it is like the weather or the seasons.

In summer, the sun shines, the temperature rises—and of course these are things to take into account when planning any activity. But to say that the sun is shining doesn't guarantee there won't be local thundershowers, or that it won't get chilly at night in the mountains. I have seen it snow in June.

The point is that there is a good deal of variety within the set of circumstances described collectively as the season. To be consistently comfortable in all seasons, I had to be selective. I couldn't get warm in someone else's sunshine. I couldn't keep dry under an "average" umbrella. I needed my own and I wanted it to be automatic.

The automatic umbrella that kept me dry during many market wet seasons, several real downpours, and the flood of May, 1962, was the *stop-loss order*.

The box theory, with its little brother, the stop-loss order, started making real money for me in the fall of 1957, when I was on my two-year dancing tour of the world. The pay-off stock was called LORILLARD. I had never heard of it. Performing at the *Arc En-Ciel* in Saigon, I had not heard, either, of the cancer scare that was about to produce a boom in filter-tip cigarettes in the United States.

The only thing about the stock that caught my attention was its performance. "The market" was depressed, but I didn't need any high-priced expert to tell me that. It was evident from the performance of the vast majority of stocks listed in *Barron's*. They were declining. Except LORILLARD. Almost alone on the Big Board it was pushing up, up, up.

Checking back, I found that it had risen in a short time from 17 all the way to 27 on a steadily rising volume—nearly 127,000 shares for the first week of October, as compared with a weekly volume of about 10,000 earlier in the year.

LORILLARD had by this time established itself in a narrow 24/27 box. Judging by past performances, I decided that it would probably be good for a run of at least three or four points—if it could break 27. So when

LORILLARD was still merrily bouncing up and down in its box, firmly resisting the down trend elsewhere, I sent a cable to my broker ordering 200 shares of LORIL-LARD buy on-stop at 27½ with a 26 stop-loss.

It will be seen from the above order that I was not, at this time, adhering strictly to the box theory. If I had, I would have placed the stop-loss much closer to the purchase price. But I had not entirely worked out the method, and thought it would be well to leave a little leeway for false movements.

Even so, the stock unexpectedly *did* reverse itself for a day, and I was sold out at 26. The same day it bounced back to 26¾.

It was a discouraging experience, but the rise continued, and I was so sure that I was right in principle that I bought back in again at 28¾.

Events vindicated the decision. By December LORIL-LARD was established in a new 31/35 box. In January it started to push up again. By now, I had completed an engagement in Bangkok and was headed for Japan, but I was still able to see all that I needed to know about the market in *Barron's* (sent to me by air and usually arriving only a few days late) and in daily cables from my broker, giving quotations on the stocks in which I was currently interested.

In Tokyo I cabled my broker to buy 400 more shares of LORILLARD. The shares were bought at 35 and 36½.

The rise continued, bouncing all the way up to 44⅜ before LORILLARD met its first major setback. On

February 19 it suddenly fell to a low of 36¾ before closing at 37¾, reflecting a brief panic set off by an adverse report on the efficacy of filter tips. Worried that the drop would go farther, I immediately cabled New York and raised my stop-loss to 36.

The dip proved to have been a fluke. The price rose and, on the strength of the action, I bought 400 more shares—this time at 38⅝. By March LORILLARD was firmly in a 50/54 box, and I raised my stop-loss on the 1,000 shares which I now owned to 49.

The total cost of the stock, at prices ranging from 28¾ to 38⅝ was $35,827.50, but the last three purchases had been on margin, which enabled me to keep a good part of my working capital for other ventures.

LORILLARD maintained its push for a few more weeks, and then began to lose steam. In mid-May, seeing that it was not acting as vigorously as I wished and that the trading volume had fallen off, I decided to sell and put the money elsewhere. My stop-loss was sure protection against any important loss. But on the other hand, I felt that I was losing money merely by standing still.

The 1,000 shares were sold for an average price of 57⅜. The total came to $56,880.45. Profit: $21,052.95.

Meanwhile, my confidence in the box theory had been strengthened by another application of it. The stock was DINERS' CLUB, then beginning to enjoy a big vogue in the United States. My first purchase was 500 shares at 24½, quickly followed by the purchase of

171

another 500 shares at 26⅛. DINERS' CLUB rapidly moved up through an almost perfect series of boxes—28/30, then 32/36, and finally, in late March, to 36¼/40 . I had raised my stop-loss weapon, meantime, to the closest fraction below the bottom of the last box, 36⅜.

After a period of indecision, interest in DINERS' CLUB began to wane, and in the last week of April the bottom of the box was penetrated and I was sold out. Price less commissions: $35,848.85. Profit: $10,328.05.

With the profits from LORILLARD and DINERS' CLUB, I was prepared for real action, and quickly found it. The new stock was E. L. BRUCE, which had begun to show an astonishing volume of sales in April, 1958, and by May was being traded at the rate of well over 75,000 shares weekly, with the price rising, in two months, from 18 all the way up to 50.

By now I had enough capital for a real flyer. My purchases in May were:

500 shares *E. L. Bruce* at 50¾
500 shares *E. L. Bruce at* 51⅛
500 shares *E. L. Bruce* at 51¾
500 shares *E. L. Bruce* at 52¾
500 shares *E. L. Bruce* at 53⅝

The total price for 2,500 shares was $130,687.55, but since I was working on a 50 per cent margin, the actual cash investment was about half of that figure.

There was a great deal going on behind the scenes during this period, affecting the price of BRUCE, but I knew nothing of it. All I knew was what *Barron's* and

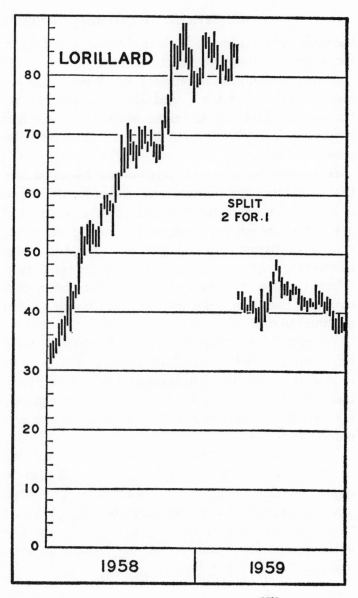

LORILLARD

SPLIT
2 FOR·1

1958   1959

the daily cables from my brokers—by now I had three, for reasons of discretion—told me.

Thus I was almost thrown for a loss when I received a telephone call at the Grand Hotel in Calcutta, informing me that the American Stock Exchange had suddenly suspended trading in BRUCE. The price by now was 77.

It seemed, one of my brokers told me by telephone, that a fight was in progress for control of the company. A New York manufacturer named Edward Gilbert and a group of associates were busily buying up stock, creating a tremendous volume of trading, and also stimulating a great deal of short-selling on the part of traders who had been unaware of the corporation struggle. They could not believe that the price could continue to rise.

When it did continue to rise, the short-sellers were forced to get back in and buy BRUCE at any price to redeem the stock they had borrowed. The result was a mad situation, in which the Amex governors ultimately decided that it was impossible to assure an orderly market in the stock.

The suspension of trading did not, of course, solve the problem of the short-sellers. They still had to repay their borrowings. That meant they had to go into the over-the-counter market and buy BRUCE at whatever price they could get it for. The over-the-counter price was already at 100. My broker's question was: Do you want to sell?

It was literally a $100,000 question—that was roughly my profit at the time. It was also a question of principle. If my theory was correct, then there could be no possible reason (except for a need for cash) to sell a rising stock.

I decided to hold. The price continued to rise. Since the stock was now in the over-the-counter market, I had no stop-loss security. Various brokers were making offers, each higher than the last. When it looked as though we had reached a price plateau, I began to sell, 100 or 200 shares at a time. The price for the entire 2,500 shares came to $427,500.00—an average of $171 per share.

My profit: $295,305.45. I had cracked the big time and confirmed the validity of my system. Bigger deals were ahead, but none could give me more satisfaction than this one.

The BRUCE power struggle ultimately made international headlines, and it is a fascinating story from start to finish. In the debacle, Edward Gilbert was cleaned out, while I—thanks to my system and a little bit of luck—came off with winnings that amounted to a respectable fortune.

I continued to test and refine the box theory at every step of the way in a long series of transactions, of which my coup in THIOKOL, previously mentioned, was the greatest, netting me some $862,000.00 in one swoop.

What I learned as I went along was that the closer I stuck to my theory, the more I earned and the less I worried. When I deviated, I was invariably wrong. This was particularly true as the tide of the market began to turn and the first faint seismic indications of the May, 1962, collapse began to be felt, as early as a year before the slump.

Increasingly I found that the stocks I bought were not progressing upward through their new upper boxes as they should have been doing. With lessening demand for common stocks, the new upper boxes became less frequent. To compensate for the erratic movements, I was tempted to set my stop-losses lower —to rely more on judgment and on hunches.

Systems must be compatible with the people who use them. What works for one temperament does not do at all for another. And there is, in the stock market as elsewhere, room for a certain amount of inspired guesswork.

Nevertheless, there is a price to be paid when inspiration fails. And on occasion I paid it.

For example, having made a handsome profit on Lorillard, I had nothing but kindly feelings about it. I was naturally drawn back to the stock which had given me such satisfactory winnings. Here is the result:

On three separate occasions, thinking that LORILLARD was about to start another run, I tried my luck. The first time I bought 1,000 shares at 70½ and was sold out at 67⅞, for a loss of $3,590.76. Nothing daunted, I tried again, buying 500 shares at 69⅛. I was sold out at 67¾. Stubbornly convinced that I had been right, I tried again, buying 1,000 shares at 67¾, this time setting my stop-loss close to the purchase price, determined that I would cut my loss to the minimum if my judgment on the timing again proved wrong. It was a good thing that I did, because I was promptly sold out at 67.

My total loss on these three operations amounted to $6,472. The experience cured me of my attachment to a "favorite" stock. I could not afford to keep pets in the stock market.

I should also have seen the implications of the later LORILLARD experience as related to my use of the stop-loss: the more rigidly it was applied, the less loss I suffered. Compare, for instance, the loss of $3,590 on the first purchase with only $1,712 on the third. In each case I bought 1,000 shares. The difference was that in one case I allowed a margin of more than 2 points; in the other, a difference of only ¾ between the purchase price and stop-loss.

So common sense tells me to *put the stop-loss as close to the bottom of the box as possible.*

In certain instances, I chose to make allowance for what I think of as the "personality" of stocks. Not all behave exactly alike. Some develop distinct personalities and, like prima donnas of the stage, become eccentric. But there are limits to eccentricity, too. Up to a point, one makes allowance for deviations. After that, one says politely, "Well, madame, I am afraid I cannot afford you. You are not compatible with my box system, and so—adieu."

By the autumn of 1961, it seemed that I was saying adieu to all of my stocks, some of them on very brief acquaintance indeed. One after the other would be closed out. Sometimes, the same stocks would show signs of recovery; and I would buy back in, only to have the door slammed in my face again.

In this way I parted with:

ZENITH RADIO (before its split), bought at 163, and sold out at 157; purchased again at 192¾, and again stopped-out, at 187¼.

CENCO INSTRUMENTS, bought at 72, sold at 69⅛; and currently around 42, after dropping all the way to 28¼.

It may surprise you to know—but nevertheless it is so—that in 1961 I was still learning, or re-learning, my lesson. My losses were even greater then, because stock movements were more uncertain. Although many issues were still in the process of beating their way to new, record highs, professional traders must have been beginning to feel that the boom could not last. The result was much short selling, and continual profit-taking—all of which made for an upward movement in uneven spurts, with many zigs, zags, and sudden retreats along the way.

For instance, in making a pilot purchase of 100

shares of M.C.A. in May of 1961, I bought on-stop at $67\frac{1}{2}$ and was sold out at $65\frac{3}{4}$. The actual cash loss was not great but I did surrender $1\frac{3}{4}$ points per share. If I had bought 1,000 shares instead of 100, the loss would have been $1,750.

In a similar situation in September of the same year, I bought 300 shares of MEAD JOHNSON at $181\frac{3}{4}$, and was stopped out at $169\frac{1}{2}$. I had deliberately set the stop-loss low, reasoning that a fluctuation of 12 points or so was not great on a stock in that price range, representing a movement of only about 5 per cent. Still, the loss was not inconsiderable—$3,600.

There were others on the loss list and, when it seemed to be growing longer with no improvement in sight, I simply stopped buying. By January, 1962, I was entirely out of the market, without a single stock to my account, nor a single prospect in mind.

Something had gone wrong. Stockbrokers, the touts of the Wall Street casino, the investment forecasting services, were still talking about a bull market; and the Dow Jones industrial average was well up in the 700's, reaching for an all-time high. But, according to my experience, the intermediate bear market had arrived. Nothing was going into new higher boxes. Prices were already too high to permit the sort of rapid growth on which my personal fortune had been made. There was nothing to do but take a breathing spell and see what would happen next.

I do not mean to take credit for realizing this.

It was not a question of acumen on my part, nor of any gift of prophecy. My box system—with its automatic closeout feature—had done the work for me. The market itself, through its own behavior, had flashed the danger signal by automatically tripping the circuit breakers which stopped-out each of my selections at the point where the price trend began to go into reverse.

That is why when the May crash came I had been out of the market for months and could read the headlines tranquilly as I drank the Planter's Punch in the Oak Bar at the Plaza.

That was when I realized that the best part of the system which I had so painstakingly devised was not that it had made my fortune. What was infinitely more important—it had enabled me to *keep* it!

CHAPTER EIGHT

Figuring My Winnings

SAD TO SAY, there is no guarantee about anything relating to the stock market except the fact that—to quote J. P. Morgan again—"It will fluctuate."

The fluctuations are caused by the same factors that makes horse races possible—differences of opinion. Some speculators think that OTIS ELEVATOR will go up; others think it will go down. They place their bets accordingly, and it is these wagers that *make* it go up or down.

As for me, I try to watch the action closely, and see which way it is actually going, before I place my bet.

I know many people who started with a lot of money and parlayed it into more in the casino. I started with a $3,000 stake in my first venture and made substantial profits. At a party recently, a young dancer cornered me. "Aren't you Nick Darvas who wrote that stock market book?" Then she asked me for information. She said that a dancer's career was a "bit feast and faminish" in her words and she was considering going into the market. "Listen," I told her, "if you can't afford to put $5,000 on the table, you can't afford to play." She was miffed at my attitude, and walked away. I said to myself: "Nick, don't be a gardener for everyone. Tend to your own greenery." I decided I had to enter the casino alone, play as a loner and leave as a loner—and I hoped a winner!

My method has been successful so far. I gamble, yes. But I gamble with the caution born of experience. One thing I know: if I'm burned by something, I stay away from it. I've had very bad results from cheap stock. Losses, losses, losses. And high commissions to boot.

The performance of the cheapies for my purpose is too irregular: the floor traders who deal in these stocks, paying no commission, are hit-and-run artists, sharpshooting for an eighth of a point here, a quarter of a point there. The effect is to create a ragged chart, and unstable boxes. Traders do not trifle with the more expensive stocks in quite the same way—they have more regard for them. Consequently, the rises and declines are more orderly and easier to observe.

My goal was to hit stocks that would make the biggest possible percentage gains; because I have long realized that I can't always hit right. Therefore, what

I must do is to manage my speculations in such a way
that when I lose, I lose only a little; and when I win,
I win big!

The stop-loss order is my principal weapon when it
comes to reducing the losses. Close application of the
box theory is the only system I know for choosing winners and, so far, it has served me very well.

My box theory and stop-loss order continue to work
very well for me, as for example in this recent transaction:

The stock was the powerful CONTROL DATA.

Back in April, 1963, I noted that CONTROL DATA was
showing signs of increasing activity, both in volume
and in rising price. The low for the year was 36. By
early May it was up to 51¼. Checking in Standard &
Poor's index, I found that the stock had come all the
way up from a low of 19 the previous year. And it was
now within fractions of its historic peak, which
was 52.

It looked like a winner, and I should have kept
closer track of it. Unfortunately, I had to go to Paris
on business for a few weeks, and I was occupied with
other matters.

When I returned, I found that CONTROL DATA had
already burst through its former ceiling, and was pushing steadily on up. Since there was no way to know
how long the run would last, there was nothing to do
but wait until it leveled off and established a new box.

When I thought I had it, I put in an on-stop pur-

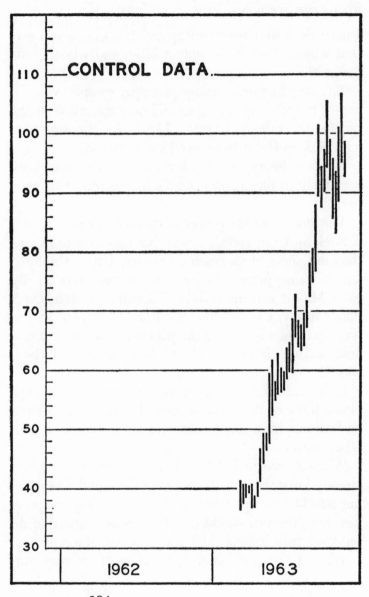

CONTROL DATA

chase order to buy 500 shares at 63, and set my stop-loss order at 62½, a fraction below what I considered to be the current ceiling.

On June 25, my broker wired me as follows:

BOUGHT 500 CD AT 63 ON STOP, SOLD 500 CD AT 62½ ON STOP

The price during the day actually had reached a high of 63¾ before slipping back. Convinced that the setback was temporary, I put the order through again. And again I was sold out! But the setback was even briefer this time. CONTROL DATA bounded upward immediately, after the single sale that had tripped my stop-loss order, and I decided to stick with it, positive that I was right.

My broker's evening report by telegram for July 5 read

BOUGHT 500 CD 65⅞ ON STOP

followed by a notation which informed me that the stock had closed at 68½. After reaching a high for the day of 68⅝ CONTROL DATA was off and running. Friday's closing price was 68⅝. On Monday it was pushing over 71, with no ceiling in sight.

I did well on the CONTROL DATA sale. And it only proved again to me that I had found an answer—perhaps a system to the lottery. Hundred per cent foolproof? No. But for me the best way.

I found that I could walk into the casino with the

odds against me, the place filled with dealers, touts and croupiers, all out to see that I played quietly, did not make a scene and did not win too often . . . and *yet* come out a WINNER.

Wall Street is not for everyone. It is certainly not for the man who cannot afford to lose. If I can't afford to take losses, I have no business at the gambling table or at the Casino of Wall Street.

Wall Street is not a philanthropic organization. I walk into the Casino with my eyes open as I would if I were walking into a Casino in Las Vegas. I ignore the chatter, I watch the action; and, I try my luck.

Index of Stocks